Ibn Battuta in Black Africa

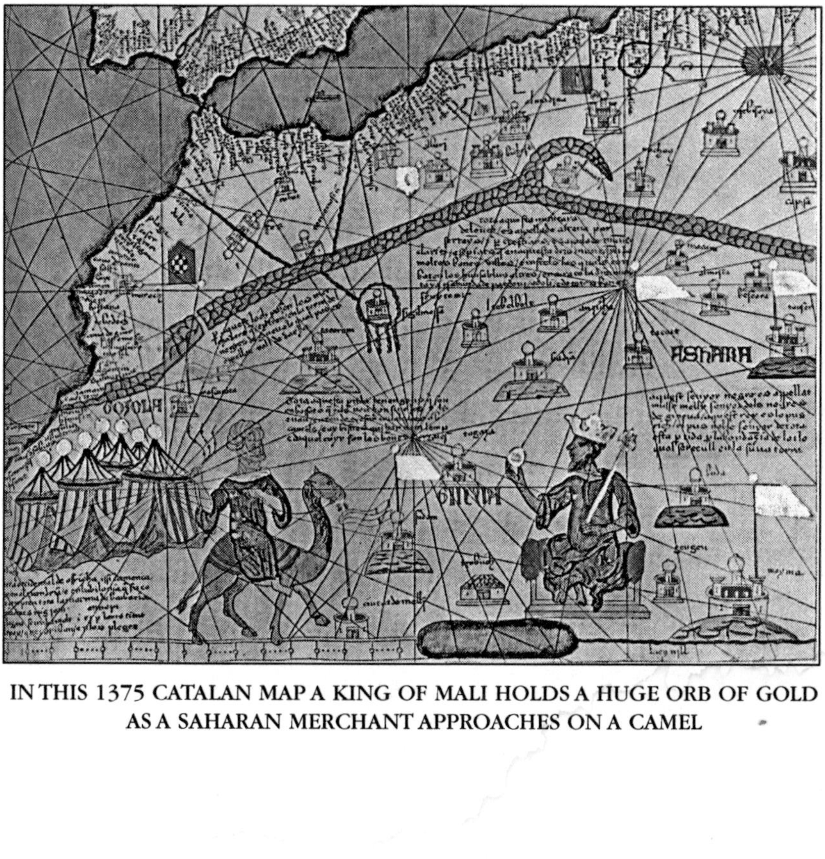

IN THIS 1375 CATALAN MAP A KING OF MALI HOLDS A HUGE ORB OF GOLD AS A SAHARAN MERCHANT APPROACHES ON A CAMEL

IN MEMORY OF

S. H. BONSU ABBAN

A DIVINITY STUDENT OF THE UNIVERSITY COLLEGE
OF GHANA WHO DIED IN AN AIR CRASH
WHILE TRAVELLING TO BRING BETTER UNDERSTANDING
BETWEEN WEST AND EAST

STREET SIGN IN TANGIER LEADING TO WHERE IBN BATTUTA IS TRADITIONALLY BELIEVED TO BE BURIED
(Photo by Ross E. Dunn)

Ibn Battuta in Black Africa

by

Said Hamdun and Noël King

With a New Foreword
by Ross E. Dunn

Expanded edition in honor of Ibn Battuta's 700th birthday

Markus Wiener Publishers
Princeton

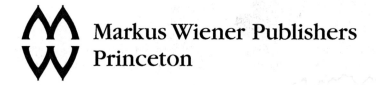

Updated and expanded edition
Fourth printing 2010

For information write to:
Markus Wiener Publishers
231 Nassau St., Princeton, NJ 08542
www.markuswiener.com

Library of Congress Cataloging-in-Publication Data

Ibn Batuta, 1304-1377.
[Tuhfat al-nuzzar fi ghara'ib al-amsar wa-'aja'ib al-asfar. English. Selections]
Ibn Battuta in Black Africa / by Said Hamdun and Noel King ; with a new foreword by Ross E. Dunn.
Previously published: Princeton: Markus Wiener, 1994.
Includes bibliographical references and index.
ISBN-13: 978-1-55876-335-7 (hc)
ISBN-10: 1-55876-335-X (hc)
ISBN-13: 978-1-55876-336-4 (pbk; alk. paper)
ISBN-10: 1-55876-336-8 (pbk; alk. paper)
1. Africa, Eastern—Description and travel—Early works to 1800. 2. Africa, West—Description and travel—Early works to 1800. 3. Ibn Batuta, 1304-1377. I. Hamdun, Said. II. King, Noel Quinton. III. Title.
DT365.2.I262513 2004
916.704/21 22

2004054224

Markus Wiener Publishers books are printed in the United States of America on acid-free paper, and meet the guidelines for permanence and durability of the Committee on Production Guidelines for Book Longevity of the Council on Library Resources.

Contents

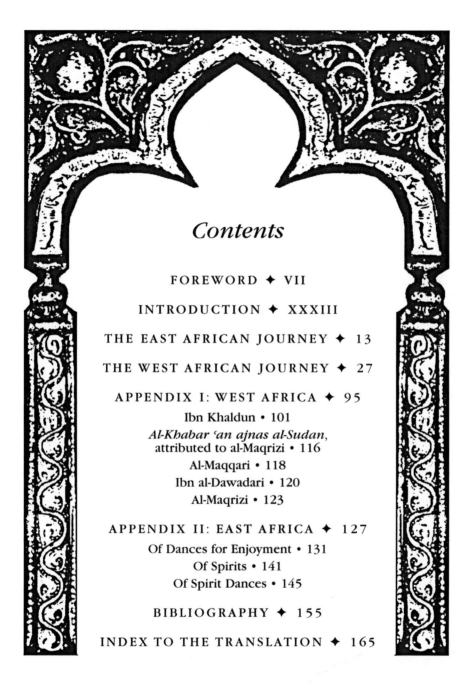

FOREWORD
by Ross E. Dunn

TRAVELERS ARRIVING IN TOWN (BAGHDAD 635 A.H./1237 A.D.)

In 1325 A.D. the young legal scholar Abu Abdallah ibn Battuta set out from his native city of Tangier on the north coast of Morocco to make the holy pilgrimage to Mecca. "I braced my resolution to quit all my dear ones," he tells us in his celebrated *Rihla,* or Book of Travels. "I set out alone, having neither fellow-traveler in whose companionship I might find cheer nor caravan whose party I might join."[1] His departure may have been poignant, but his loneliness did not last long. Within a few days he was meeting all sorts of people on the road, and as he traveled back and forth across the Eastern Hemisphere during the ensuing twenty-nine years, he made hundreds of friends, married numerous women, fathered several children, and counted among his associates eminent scholars, royal officials, rich merchants, and Mongol kings.

Indeed, one of the more fascinating aspects of Ibn Battuta's travels through the equivalent of nearly fifty modern countries is that he was repeatedly running into people he knew. Wandering lost in the remote forests of northern Turkey, he met up with "an acquaintance," who saved him and his traveling companions from perishing in a snowstorm. When he tried to make a visit *incognito* to the Maldive Islands in the Indian Ocean, travelers who had known him in northern India 1,600 miles away recognized him and blew his cover. In southern China he met a man named al-Bushri whom he had known slightly in India and who came originally from a town in Morocco only forty miles from Tangier. About five and a half years later when he was traveling in the northern Sahara Desert at the opposite extremity of the hemisphere, he became the house guest of al-Bushri's brother! (See p. 30.)

In the age of the global village we might not be terribly surprised to bump into some old acquaintance while changing planes in Tokyo or Frankfurt. But six and a half centuries ago, when the world's population was many times less than it is now, cities were much smaller and more widely scattered, vast deserts and oceans separated settled communities, and the pace of travel was limited to the speed of horses or sailing ships, we might suppose that few people ever ventured far beyond their natal land.

In fact the caravan trails and sea lanes of the fourteenth century hummed with travelers on long-distance errands of all sorts. Among travelers, moreover, Muslims were preeminent. Because the lands of Islam dominated the center of the Eastern Hemisphere and extended nearly all the way across it, Muslim merchants moved incessantly here and there among the major regions of Eurasia and Africa carrying the greater part of the hemisphere's international trade in luxury and everyday goods. Other Muslims went abroad to make the holy pilgrimage (*hajj*) to Mecca and Medina in Arabia, a journey that might take a poor pilgrim several years. Still others traveled as diplomatic emissaries, imperial messengers, wandering mystics, or cultured

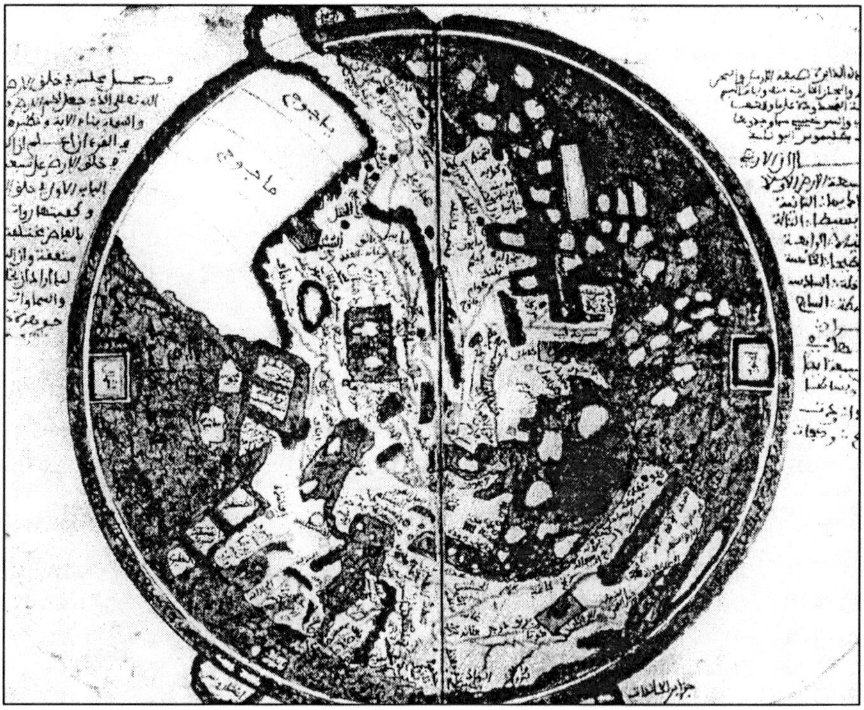

ARAB WORLD MAP BY IBN SAID, 13TH CENTURY

scholars in search of books and famous teachers.

Islamic civilization was highly cosmopolitan in the fourteenth century in two respects. First, Islamic cities had on the whole the most heterogenous populations of residents and transient visitors of any cities in the world. This was especially true of cities of the Islamic heartland partly because the region between Egypt and Persia (what we call today the Middle East) was geographically the narrow bottleneck of the hemisphere (semi-arid steppes to the north, deserts and seas to the south) and therefore the funnel through which all the east-west trade routes passed. A diverse assortment of transients and temporary residents—Arabs, Persians, Jews, Kurds, Berbers, Turks, Greeks, Italians, and Catalans—walked the streets of Damascus, Aleppo, Jerusalem, Tabriz, Alexandria, and, most cosmopolitan of all in Ibn Battuta's time, Cairo.

Islamic internationalism was also evidenced in the collective life of the *'ulama*, the class of Muslim religious and legal scholars. In Islamic belief individuals who traveled to make the *hajj* or to further their education in the religious sciences were thought to merit divine approval. Garbed in white gown and voluminous turban, the *'alim*, or pious scholar, was a common sight on the open road as he scurried from one city to another to seek out a particular legal text, study with a celebrated teacher, or attend a religiously endowed college. Moreover, because the *'ulama* were the lettered class and the guardians and interpreters of the sacred law of Islam (*shari'a*), the more skilled and gifted among them were much in demand to fill bureaucratic posts, direct religious institutions, and lead diplomatic missions. Fourteenth century Islam was a civilization not only of many cities but many kingdoms as well. Secular sultans and princes normally regarded it as their moral duty to treat lawyers and religious doctors in their service with respect and generosity. On the other hand, rulers could be fickle about whom they favored or disfavored. Consequently, ambitious and talented scholar-bureaucrats moved frequently from capital to capital in search of prestigious and lucrative posts. And if they should for some reason irritate their princely employer, they might skip town at very short notice.

The *'ulama* of the medieval centuries might collectively be described as the best-traveled and most cosmopolitan intellectual class in world history up to that time.Their primary loyalty was not to state, nation, or tribe, but to the *dar al-Islam*, or House of Islam, the lands where Muslim populations predominated or at least where Muslim communities ruled. In Ibn Battuta's time the *dar al-Islam* extended straight across the Eastern Hemisphere. Consequently, the most mobile and best educated among the scholarly class possessed a sharper universalist vision of humankind, a broader mental grasp of the inhabitied regions of Eurasia and Africa, than any other group in the world.

Lettered Muslims of North Africa or Andalusia (southern Spain) were particularly inclined to make long trips abroad, partly to fulfill the religious obligations of the *hajj*, partly to make study tours of Cairo, Damascus, and other university cities of the Middle East. From the point of view of an Egyptian or Syrian scholar, North Africa was *jazirat al-maghrib*, the "island of the west," a region of mountains and plains cut off from the center by sea and desert. Moroccan and Andalusian intellectuals were acutely conscious that they lived in the "far west." A journey to the center was an opportunity to acquire books and diplomas, commune with the best scholars, and generally immerse oneself in the cosmopolitan life. North African sojourners were likely to earn both scholarly credentials and intellectual prestige in the Middle East and so return home to honorable and well-paying jobs in service to their religious community or their king.

The career of Ibn Marzuk, a contemporary of Ibn Battuta and a scholarly luminary of the century, is a notable example of the formative influence of the Middle East on a North African *'alim*. At the age of about seven, Ibn Marzuk left his native city of Tlemcen (in western Algeria) to perform the *hajj* with his father. He remained in the Middle East throughout his childhood, studying with masters in Mecca, Medina, Jerusalem, Hebron, Alexandria, and Cairo. He returned home when he was about twenty-two to launch a brilliant career in public life. Serving at different times sultans of Granada, Tunis, and Morocco, he occupied numerous posts including envoy to the king of Castile, minister of state, and mosque preacher in three cities. He studied with more than 250 teachers and authored several works in history, ethics, and law. In his later years he returned to Cairo where he served as professor, preacher, and judge. Here was a true cosmopolite of his age.

Ibn Battuta never came close to matching Ibn Marzuk's brilliance as a scholar or public official, but he was every bit an *'alim*. He came from a respected family of jurists and judges who practiced their profession in Morocco and Andalusia. His ethnic ancestors were rural Berbers of northern Morocco, but in language and culture he was a city-dwelling Arab. In his youth he learned as much of the religious and juridical sciences—Qur'anic exegesis, the traditions of the Prophet (hadith), grammar, rhetoric, theology, logic, and law—as the mosque schools of a provincial town like Tangier could offer. More important for his traveling career, he absorbed the moral and social qualities expected of an *'alim*. These included a pious and restrained demeanor; a refined sense of discretion, protocol, personal hygiene, and proper dress; an aptitude for clever and learned conversation. From his accounts of personal experience in the *Rihla*, it is evident that even though he had no profound intellectual gifts, he was, to use the modern phrase, a "class act."

The second quarter of the fourteenth century was the twilight of the age of Mongol dominance, the extraordinary period of about a century and a half when Mongol kings, first the conqueror Chinggis Khan and then his sons and grandsons, ruled the greater part of the Eurasian land mass. At the time of Ibn Battuta's travels the unified empire of Chinggis had already broken into four Mongol successor kingdoms, all of them enormous in their own right. These four states were well-administered and reasonably stable, and their rulers continued in the best Mongol tradition to protect the long-distance trade routes and encourage merchants of all faiths and nations to use them. Moreover, even where Mongol lords did not reign, strong, commerce-minded states were the rule in the early fourteenth century. These included, among others, the Marinid kingdom of Morocco, the Mamluk Sultanate of Egypt and Syria, the Delhi Sultanate of northern India, and the Mali empire in West Africa. The existence of this chain of robust states stretching all the way across Eurasia and deep into Africa meant that inter-regional trade boomed, not only on the overland caravan trails but also on the maritime routes of the southern seas.

In other words, the second quarter of the fourteenth century was a relatively auspicious time for an adventurous Muslim to

MONGOL RULER WITH AN ARAB SCRIBE (CA. 710 A.D./1310 A.D.)

make an extended tour of the world. A traveling scholar could always hitch a ride with a caravan, and anyone who was traveling in connection with the *hajj*, whether he had any money or not, could always find rest and refreshment in a caravansary, mosque, or private home. Ironically, Ibn Battuta's career neared its end just as this relatively halcyon period was coming to a close. In 1347 the Black Death swept into the Middle East, North Africa, and Europe, heralding a half century of economic troubles, political collapse, and social upheaval that seemed to afflict nearly every part of the Eastern Hemisphere. Ibn Battuta survived the plague (though his mother did not), and he settled into the quiet, comfortable life of a judge in some provincial Moroccan town, safe from the international calamities occurring all around.

The Moroccan may have been the greatest traveler of his era, but he was not an aimless wanderer. His motives for going to particular places varied. First of all, he traveled, like tens of thousands of Muslims in the fourteenth century, to perform the rites of the *hajj* at the holy places of Mecca in western Arabia. He left home, he tells us, "swayed by an overmastering impulse within me and a desire long-cherished in my bosom to visit these illustrious sancturaries"[2]. In the course of his career he participated in the rituals of the *hajj* season six or seven times, each time presumably accruing divine merit. Indeed, Mecca became the hub of his tours. During most of his years on the road he was either traveling away from Arabia or returning to it.

Second, he traveled, as so many *'ulama* did, to pursue advanced studies in Islamic law, though in fact he never put much time into them. With the exception of a few months of study with teachers in Damascus (and possibly more time in Mecca), he never settled into the routine of listening to lectures and mastering learned texts, which was the only route to genuine intellectual proficiency.

Third, he traveled as a devotee of Sufism, which was the mystical, ecstatic dimension of Islam. Through Sufi learning and practice the individual sought personal communion with God, usually under the guidance of a saintly master. In the fourteenth century Sufi ideas and practices were becoming fully incorporated into Islamic orthodoxy, very notably in North Africa. Ibn

Battuta journeyed to a number of places specifically to visit living scholar-saints who possessed an abundance of *baraka*, the quality of divine grace that might be imparted to disciples and devotees. He reports in the *Rihla* that on several occasions he was tempted to settle down to a life of Sufi spirituality, though the lure of the road invariably overpowered him.

Fourth, he traveled to seek employment and generous rewards in government service. He almost certainly lacked the scholarly credentials to secure a worthy post as a jurist in a city such as Cairo or Damascus, where brilliant lawyers abounded and the competition was stiff. However, in the further lands where Islamic civilization was newer and rougher-edged and where educated cadres were in short supply, rulers were less choosy about the intellectual "résumés" of the people they employed. Ibn Battuta also commanded a certain prestige in countries such as India simply because he was an Arab and therefore a man of "the Prophet's race." He spent about eight years (1334-1341) in the Sultanate of Delhi, an Islamic kingdom of Turkic origin that had only been founded a little more than a century before his arrival. He served first as a judge, then as an administrator of a royal mausoleum, and finally as the sultan's ambassador to the Mongol court of China, though this last commission was aborted following a shipwreck off the coast of India. Later, he served for several months as chief judge in the Maldive Islands, a tiny Islamic state in the Indian Ocean.

Ibn Battuta also traveled to some places for no concrete reason at all, only to satisfy his curiosity, have an adventure, or perhaps to satisfy a prideful goal to see more of the *dar al-Islam* than anyone else ever had. In the *Rihla* he reports that he met a learned man in western Turkey who was particularly well-traveled. He takes pains, however, to list the several countries that this man had not visited and he had. "I have outdone him," he crows, "by visiting these regions."

Ibn Battuta's two trips to Africa south of the Sahara occupied only a small part of his nearly three-decade career. His sea voyage from Arabia to the coasts of East Africa and back took him only about five months (the first part of 1329 or 1331, depending how one interprets the *Rihla's* chronological clues). His journey by camel caravan from Morocco to the Mali empire in West Africa, his last recorded adventure, lasted about two years (1352-1354). Even so, his narratives of these two journeys have a historical value far out of proportion to their place in his overall itinerary. The *Rihla* represents the only eye-witness account we have of both the East African city-states and the Mali empire in the fourteenth century, or for that matter the thirteenth as well. Other Arab scholars of the period compiled and reported information on these two regions, but they relied on second-hand accounts of merchants or other travelers who never wrote their own books about what they saw. Ibn Battuta's account of the East African cities of Mogadishu, Mombasa, and Kilwa is informative on a number of historical points but also brief. His report on Mali is four times longer and much richer, including detailed descriptions of the royal government. We owe Ibn Battuta a deep debt for bearing witness to the magnitude and brilliance of this grassland empire.

About twenty-three years separated Ibn Battuta's trips to East and West Africa, and each one was linked to an entirely different circuit of travel. The commercial towns stretching along the tropical coasts of what are today Somalia, Kenya, Zanzibar, Tanzania, and Mozambique belonged to the intercommunicating world of the Indian Ocean. In Ibn Battuta's time they were thoroughly Muslim towns with close economic and cultural connections to South Arabia and the lands of the Persian Gulf. Morever, the seasonal monsoon winds, which permitted sailing ships to cross open expanses of the Indian Ocean with reasonable safety and cost efficiency, connected East Africa and its commerce not only to the Middle East but also to India and ultimately China.

In the fourteenth century there may have been about forty settlements along the coast from Mogadishu southward. Except for enslaved captives and traders coming in from the East African interior, the inhabitants of the towns were Muslims. Since the early centuries of Islam, Arab or Persian merchants and other adventurers had been visiting the coast, many remaining permanently and intermarrying with local African families. The rulers and wealthy merchants of the larger ports made a point of tracing their descent from Muslim "pioneers" who had come from the heartland of Islamic civilization. However, the towns were fundamentally African; they were not Middle Eastern settler colonies. To illustrate the point, Swahili, the most widely spoken language in East Africa today, was in the fourteenth century evolving into the principal language of trade and everyday affairs along the coast. Swahili incorporates numerous linguistic borrowings from Arabic, notably religious

A DHOW UNDER SAIL OFF THE COAST OF EAST AFRICA

or political words, but it is fundamentally a Bantu African language.

The more important coastal towns imported quantities of luxury goods such as Indian cottons, Persian glassware, and Chinese pottery that contributed to the agreeable urban life-style of the richer households. These families, who lived in comfortable stone homes or even ornate palaces, made their fortunes mainly by exporting African products, particularly ivory, ambergris, mangrove poles, slaves, and gold. In those times the overland trade, which ran hundreds of miles into the interior, was in the hands of corporations of non-Muslim African merchants who brought goods down to the coast for transshipment. In other words, the towns would never have thrived as they did were it not for the production and commercial enterprise of the inland populations. Even so, the inhabitants of these diminutive city-states cared most about their complex economic and cultural connections with the wider world of Islam. Travelers were incessantly sailing back and forth between the coast and the northerly ports of the Arabian Sea. Ibn Battuta would not have found his voyage more than 800 miles south of the equator a particularly exotic experience.

But why did he go to East Africa? He offers no explicit motive in the *Rihla*. It is possible that when he sailed from Jidda, Mecca's port on the Red Sea, to Aden, one of the major ports of the Indian Ocean trade, he was already thinking of going to India to seek a post in the Delhi Sultanate. He arrived at Aden during a period of the annual monsoon cycle when ships would not normally have been going to India. A vessel was, however, hoisting sail for the African coast. This may have been one of those occasions when he visited a new part of the Islamic world simply because it was there.

He might well have made an extended sojourn in Mogadishu or Kilwa. The local sultans of the towns were always on the lookout for lettered Arabs from abroad who might give administrative service and lend cosmopolitan prestige to their little courts. Ibn Battuta appears to have enjoyed his voyage and was particularly impressed by the Sultan of Kilwa. "This sultan is a very humble man," the *Rihla* says. "He sits with the poor people and eats with them, and gives respect to people of religion and of prophetic descent." (p. 24) Despite the warm reception

THE RUINS OF THE GREAT MOSQUE OF KILWA

he received as one of these "people of religion," he decided to return to South Arabia as soon as he could find a ship. From there he made his way back to Mecca for another *hajj* season.

He undertook his courageous journey across the Sahara to West Africa after returning home to Morocco in 1349. He may have decided to visit Mali, despite its location on the far side of the fearsome void, simply because it was one of the few Muslim kingdoms in the world he had not seen. Some scholars speculate that Abu Inan, the Sultan of Morocco and one of the more vigorous kings of the Marinid dynasty, sent Ibn Battuta to the Sudan on a diplomatic mission. The purpose of the embassy would have been to strengthen commercial ties, particularly the gold trade, between Mali and Morocco. Such a motive is plausible. The Sultan of Delhi, after all, had chosen Ibn Battuta to lead a delegation to China. Moreover, diplomatic exchanges between the kings of Mali and their North African counterparts did occasionally take place. Ibn Battuta does mention in the *Rihla* that when he was starting his homeward journey from the southern Sahara, he received a message from Abu Inan "commanding me to appear in his sublime presence." (p. 73) On the other hand, he never states explicitly that he was traveling under orders. Since he usually reported any business he had with kings or princes in great detail, sprinkling names of the powerful and famous all over the *Rihla*, it seems likely that if Abu Inan had commissioned him to go to Mali, the traveler would have taken pains to let his readers know it. On the contrary, he berates Sulaiman, the *mansa*, or king of Mali for treating him as a person of no particular account.

Whatever Ibn Battuta's role in trans-Saharan diplomacy, there is no doubt that the Marinid government wanted Mali's trade. The auriferous mines of West Africa, which lay in savanna country near the southern frontier of the empire, supplied a large percentage of the gold that circulated in both Christian Europe and the Islamic states. Camel caravans carried it to North Africa, and from there it entered the wider Mediterranean market largely through the intermediary of Genoese, Catalan, or other European sea merchants. Indeed, the high age of the Mali kingdom from the mid-thirteenth to the mid-fourteenth centuries corresponded to the period when Europe was exchanging silver for gold as its principal hard currency. This prompted the European traders to offer higher and higher prices for gold in the North African ports. Europe's rising demand, coupled with the steady market in the Islamic states, spurred the mines to increase production. The *mansas* in turn profited immensely because they took golden tribute from the local authorities who controlled the mines, and they scrupulously taxed all caravans passing through their territory.

The merchants of Mali transshipped gold northward through towns that lay along the southern edge of the desert, notably Walata, Timbuktu, Gao, and Takadda. Like the East African cities, these towns occupied a geographic frontier, in this case the transitional zone between the great desert and the quite densely populated grassland belt of West Africa that the Arab geographers called the *bilad al-sudan*, or land of black people. The northbound caravans organized in these "ports" of the Sahara carried not only gold but also ivory, ostrich feathers, hides,

EXPORT PRODUCTS FROM MALI: IVORY AND GOLD

slaves, and various other West African products. The camel trains arriving out of the desert from commercial centers at the *northern* edge of the desert, notably the Moroccan city of Sijilmasa, brought salt, textiles, horses, copper, books, paper, iron ware, spices, wheat, and a wide array of goods from the Mediterranean world.

As important as international trade was to Mali's prosperity, the economic bedrock of the empire was agriculture. Most of the subjects of the *mansas* were not town-dwellers but farmers, cattle herders, or village artisans. Mali was also an empire of considerable ethnic complexity. The core population, as well as the chiefly clan that provided the *mansas*, spoke Malinke, but peoples of diverse languages and cultural traditions paid allegiance to the imperial throne.

Mali was not the earliest large-scale West African state. Ghana had come before it but withered away in the eleventh

IN EXCHANGE FOR SALT

and twelfth centuries. The early *mansas* were regional lords of the upper valleys of the Senegal and Niger Rivers. In the thirteenth century these leaders succeeded in gaining control of territory between the gold fields of the southern savanna and the desert gateways to the north, thus positioning themselves to take tribute in gold from the populations controling the mines and to levy taxes on gold-bearing caravans. These revenues permitted the *mansas* to build up their army, which was comprised mainly of infantry bowmen and armored cavalry. As the king's forces moved east and west across the fertile savanna, more farming populations were subdued and taxed and more of the north-south flow of commerce was brought under state control. Riches flowed into the royal treasury, and the army and administration expanded even more. In the course of the thirteenth and fourteenth centuries the *mansas* extended their realm westward to the Atlantic coast, eastward past the great bend of the Niger River, and northward to the desert fringe. At some point early in the expansion of the empire the ruling family also converted to Islam. Whatever religious feeling may have motivated them, their conversion enhanced their prestige among established Muslim merchant communities of the savanna, and it opened

A MARKET NEAR THE SITE OF OLD SIJILMASA
(Photo by Ross E. Dunn)

wider possibilities for commercial and diplomatic contacts with North Africa.

Ibn Battuta had a knack for visiting Islamic kingdoms in their prime, and Mali was no exception. Just about the time he was preparing to start, Mansa Musa, the most renowned of the Mali emperors, was making his famous pilgrimage to Mecca, crossing the Sahara to Egypt with a caravan of thousands. The *mansa* and his retainers, the Arab chroniclers tell us, spread so much gold around the Cairo bazaars that for a time its price went down on the Egyptian market. Mansa Musa's undertaking of this lavish pilgrimage more than 3,500 miles from home was an indicator of the wealth, orderliness, and stability of his kingdom. Mansa Sulaiman, who came to the throne in 1341, appears to have been an equally effective ruler, though after his death in 1360 the empire gradually deteriorated.

Ibn Battuta has given us a marvelous description of Mali under Mansa Sulaiman, but he definitely had mixed feelings about the place. On the one hand he was impressed that a person could feel perfectly secure traveling hundreds of miles through the royal domains. He also regarded the Muslim population of the kingdom as pious and earnestly dedicated to their mosque prayers and Quranic studies. On the other hand, he found Sulaiman less generous toward visiting doctors of the law than he knew Mansa Musa had been. He also abhorred various local practices that he thought inconsistent with Islamic rectitude and seemliness. Women went about bare-breasted, men engaged in private conversations with women who were not their wives, subjects of the *mansa* prostrated themselves on

CARAVAN APPROACHING TIMBUKTU
(drawing by Heinrich Barth in 1853)

the ground and threw dust over their heads when they approached him. Ibn Battuta's standards were those of a cultured Arab urbanite and a righteous, if not sometimes priggish, upholder of the sacred law. He was not particularly interested in recognizing basic realities of Mali society. Most of the *mansa's* subjects were not Muslims at all but adhered to the local religions of their ancestors. Even the commercial towns were probably less thoroughly Islamicized than the East African city-states. The *mansas* incorporated Islamic rituals into their royal proceedings, they used Arabic to some extent as a language of administration, and they retained the services of numerous Muslim scribes, treasurers, and jurists, some of whom were migrants from North Africa. A few of the kings went to Mecca. On the other hand, royal legitimacy depended on the loyalty of the Malinke core population, which was largely non-Muslim and would have disapproved of any radical break with traditional cultural conventions or expections of how kings should behave. Because Islam had reached West Africa mainly from Morocco, Ibn Battuta was perhaps unprepared for these startling cultural differences between his homeland and the *bilad al-Sudan*.

In one sense Mali and the East African coast were part of two entirely different international worlds. Mali belonged to the commercial realm of the Sahara basin and the Mediterranean. East Africa looked toward the Middle East and across the sea to India. In other ways, however, both regions were very much part of the same world, the world of expanding Islam, the world of interlinked trans-hemispheric trade, the world of cosmopoli-

TOMB IN TANGIER WHERE IBN BATTUTA IS TRADITIONALLY BELIEVED TO BE BURIED
(Photo by Ross E. Dunn)

tan travelers who paid little attention to political or ethnic dividing lines.

Said Hamdun and Noël King's sprightly, informal, eminently readable translation of the *Rihla's* Arabic text seems to capture Ibn Battuta, the inquisitive, urbane cosmopolite. In these pages we discover no medieval pedant or gloomy cleric but a raconteur, a charmer, and a lover of life.

Notes

1. H.A.R. Gibb, trans. and ed., *The Travels of Ibn Battuta A.D. 1325–1354, Translated with Revisions and Notes from the Arabic Text Edited by C. Defremery and B.R. Sanguinetti* (Cambridge: Cambridge University Press for the Hakluyt Society, 1958), p. 8.

2. Gibb, *Travels*, p. 8.77

INTRODUCTION
by Said Hamdun and Noël King

LECTURE BY A FAMOUS TEACHER (IRANIAN, 16TH CENTURY)

Ibn Baṭṭūṭa, who was born at Tangier in North Africa in 1304 and died not far from there some sixty-five years later, was the greatest of the pre-modern travellers and will go down in history as being notable among the travellers of all time. Benjamin of Tudela, a Jew from Spain who in the second half of the twelfth century travelled to Baghdad and back, hardly touched central or south Asia and did not penetrate Africa. Marco Polo (1254-1324), a Christian, reached China and returned to Venice by way of south-east Asia and India, but he did not get into Africa. Chinese travellers reached Europe but did not go inland in Arabia or to West Africa, or even pass through the hinterland of Arab Africa.

On his side, ibn Baṭṭūṭa set out from his home town in North Africa at the age of twenty-one, and travelled till he was nearly fifty. He went across the countries we would today call Morocco, Algeria, Tunisia, Egypt, Israel, Lebanon and Syria, then southwards through Jordan into Arabia to Mecca. There he spent some years and from there visited Iraq and Iran as well as southern Arabia. He visited the coast of the Sudan, went back to south Arabia and from Aden went on southwards to Somalia and Tanzania. He then visited the Persian Gulf and returned to Mecca by an overland route. From there he journeyed through Egypt, Syria, Asia Minor, the Crimea and the Balkans to Constantinople; thence through southern Russia and central Asia to Afghanistan, Pakistan and India. From Delhi he went to south India and the Maldives, Ceylon, Assam and Bengal (areas now in India and Bangladesh). He journeyed on through Malaysia and Indonesia to China. On returning home to Tangier he visited Spain, and finally walked across the Sahara to ancient Malli. It is the black African section of his travels which confirms his pre-eminence, and it is this part of his narrative which is the subject of this book.

Besides the places he visited and the incredible distances he travelled on foot or on the backs of horses and camels, ibn Baṭṭūṭa is notable for the picture he gives of the Islamic world of his day. This came nearest to being the first genuinely world civilization which ever existed before the Americas and Australia were added to 'the known world'. Ibn Baṭṭūṭa as a person from a North African town could feel genuinely part of it. By descent he was Berber—and nobody knows how long ago the Berbers came to Africa—history mentions them hundreds of years before it tells of people speaking Bantu languages; they are about as African as anybody can be. By language and culture he was an Arab and a Muslim. This sharing in the world of Islam meant he could travel without money or resources and everywhere find he could understand and be understood, obtain hospitality as well as rich gifts from rulers or from Muslim merchants. It is true that in some respects Islamic civilization had passed its zenith: the Arab conquests of the first Islamic century since the migration of the Prophet to Medina in A.D. 622 had been followed up by the rise of the superb civilizations of the Maghrib (north-western Africa), Egypt, Syria, Iraq and Persia. The Empire of the Caliphs and other parts of the Islamic world had suffered much at the hands of the Mongols who took Baghdad in 1258, and, in ibn Baṭṭūṭa's own day, the Black Death was to decimate whole countrysides. But following the Mongol opening up of Central Asia, Islamic civilization was able to penetrate even more widely. The new peoples coming westwards from Central Asia of 'Turkish' background were converted, and glorious Muslim civilizations arose in Turkey and India.

In the meantime, Islam had journeyed far into Africa and South-East Asia and there were flourishing Muslim communities and outposts in West and East Africa as well as in Malaysia and Indonesia. Ibn Baṭṭūṭa sets before us a breathtaking panorama of a civilization which included or touched upon every part of the world other than the Americas and Australia. He gives us an unforgettable picture of Islamic culture, hospitality, scholarship and holiness.

As a bonus, from his own description, we learn a great deal about the man himself, in fact, there are few pre-modern people of whom we can obtain so vivid a picture. We get to know a very remarkable human being, who is somehow so real and like ourselves that soon we enter the more deeply into the narrative and see things through his eyes. He is insatiably curious and his interests are impressively wide. He is concerned not only with kings, politics, geography, routes and wealth; but also he takes an intense interest in local products, especially the food and the women. He has deep prejudices, for instance, against schismatics in Islam whose views differ from his own, and against unbelievers and rationalists. Yet reading these travels is a sure antidote to the eurocentricity of most American and European medieval historians, for here we have a writer who could view things Magribian, Egyptian, Syrian, Byzantine, Persian, Arabian, Indian, Chinese, Italian, Spanish and African with the same impartial acceptances, enjoyments and rejections.

Ibn Baṭṭūṭa has his pettinesses. He loves name-dropping: trying to impress us by reciting the names of the people whom he met or with whom he was connected in scholarly learning or holiness. Yet it was these connections which were his 'traveller's cheques' which produced funds from donors as he travelled. He loves a fine spectacle, and his pages are full of the pomp and circumstance of parades and processions. Yet his book was intended to entertain as well as instruct and, despite oneself, using ibn Baṭṭūṭa as proxy, one enjoys the triumph, the glory and the splendour of it all. This world-traveller is something of an old prude; he gets quite upset at seeing young women whose breasts had formed going round in the nude, but he is equally outraged in a men's public bath to find men bathing without loincloths.

He enjoys his dignity and comforts. He lets slip that he never travels without a slave-girl or two, and he is avaricious in his desire for rich donations from Muslim rulers and not averse to drawing their attention to their duty to give him gifts by means which fall little short of blackmail. He carefully puts down anyone who might claim to have travelled as much as he has. He does not fail to report his illnesses. He seems to have experienced most travellers' diseases from Lahore sore to Delhi belly. Only the fact that the New World had not been discovered saved him from Montezuma's revenge.

Yet ibn Baṭṭūṭa is a man of courage. He never reveals any fear of the ocean, though he did not take to sea travel till comparatively late in his career and faced some terrifying storms. He loves luxury and yet he received his calling to be a traveller almost as Saint Paul received his vocation to Apostleship. Ibn Baṭṭūṭa betrays that he would have enjoyed a regular home life and seeing his children grow up before his eyes. He was also generous to others and sensitive to their suffering, whether they were Hindu women committing *sutee* or slave-boys thirsty in the desert. For a man who is so interesting a character and who achieved so much, it is surprising how little about him his contemporaries have passed on to us.

Ibn Ḥajar of Ascalon who died in A.D. 1448 has a note about ibn Baṭṭūṭa in his *Hidden Pearls*.[1] He gives his name in full as 'Muḥammad ibn Abdallāh ibn Muḥammad ibn Ibrāhīm ibn Muḥammad ibn Ibrāhīm ibn Yūsuf of the Luwāta tribe [a Berber group] and the city of Tangier'. He says that ibn K̲h̲aṭīb remarks (to translate colloquially): 'He had not too much of what it takes.' Gibb translates this as: 'He had a modest share of the sciences.'[2] Presumably the meaning is that he was not really a scholar. The biographer gives ibn K̲h̲aṭīb's summary of ibn Baṭṭūṭa's travels and goes on to say that ibn Marzūq reported that ʿAbdallāh ibn Juzayy was told to write up the traveller's narrative by the sultan; ibn Baṭṭūṭa was suspected of telling lies but ibn Marzūq considered him innocent.[3] He also reports that he lived on till the seventieth year of the eighth Muslim century (A.D. 1368-1369), and died while serving as *qāḍi* in some town or another. He remarks on his pre-eminence as a traveller and adds that he was a very generous and gracious person.

The only other contemporary material we have is to be found in ibn K̲h̲aldūn's *Muqaddimah*.[4] He says that when ibn Baṭṭūṭa, a shaikh from Tangier, returned to the Maghrib after twenty years of travel, he told many stories, especially about India. It was suspected that he was a liar, but ibn Khaldūn consulted one of the court officials who told him of a man who was put in prison with his son and the boy grew up therein. The lad asked his father about the animals whose flesh was served to them—mutton, beef, camel-meat. However well his father described them, for the boy sheep, cows and camels were only types of rat, for rats were the only animals he had seen.

Bearing this salutary parable in mind, we too must ask to what extent we can trust this narrative. It is clear that now and then ibn Baṭṭūṭa succumbs to every traveller's or raconteur's temptation to embellish his narrative. Thus, when he had reached the Black Sea, he gives a rather suspicious narrative of a visit to Bulghar in which he covered about a thousand miles in less than two weeks. When travelling in far eastern seas on the way to China he tells of a visit to a state which is ruled by women; historians find great difficulty in locating it. On the way back from China he tells of a storm after which they saw a shape like a mountain and his companions said it was the *ruq*, an enormous bird which would destroy them if it saw them. Luckily the wind changed and they got away. Even so, he does not actually say he saw it. These are the most notable examples in the whole narrative, and even with them it is cruel to compare him with Gulliver, though the *ruq* may just remind us of Sindbad.

In the main, ibn Baṭṭūṭa himself is one of the most reliable sources that has come down to us from pre-modern times. To say this is not to guarantee everything in the *Travels*. A traveller

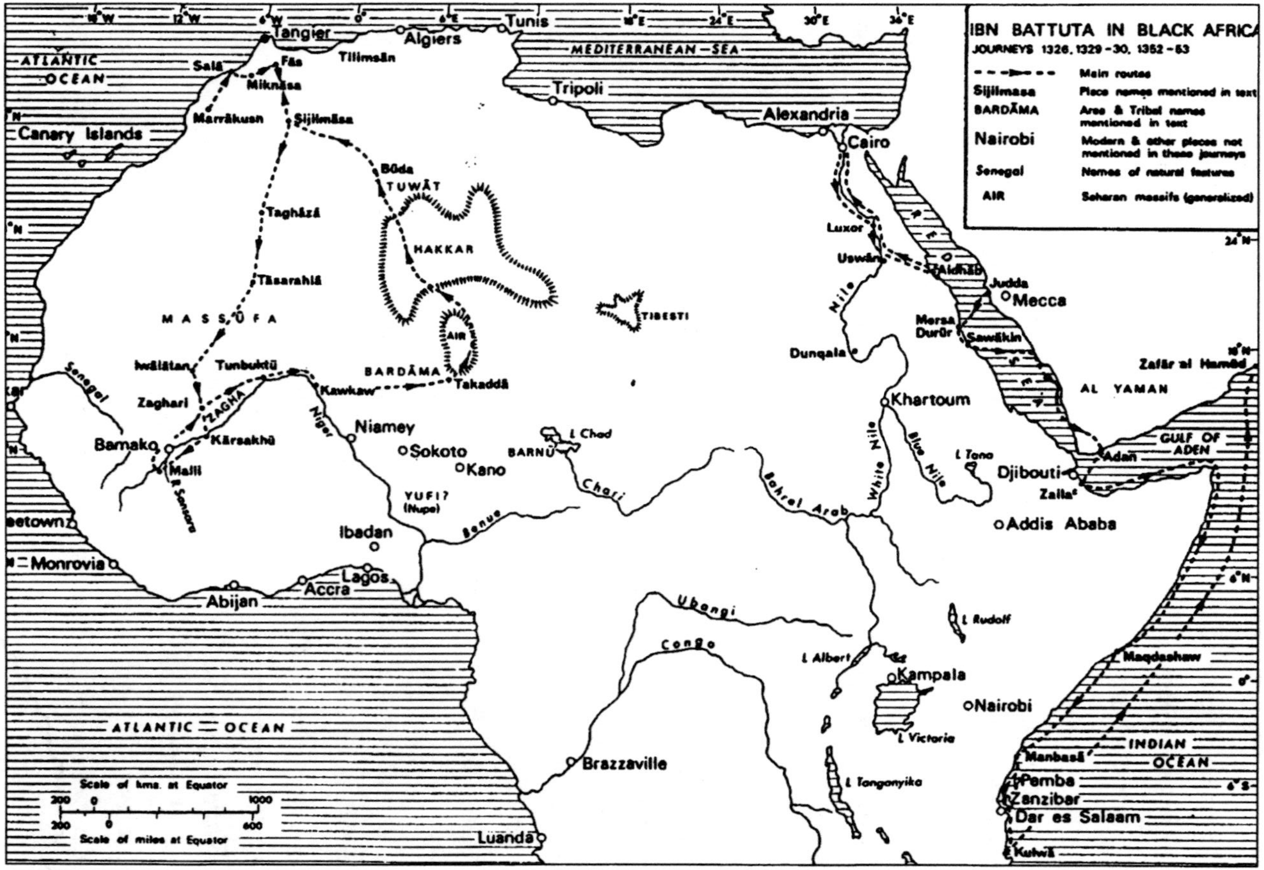
IBN BATTUTA IN BLACK AFRICA
JOURNEYS 1326, 1329-30, 1352-53
Main routes
Sijilmasa Place names mentioned in text
BARDĀMA Area & Tribal names mentioned in text
Nairobi Modern & other places not mentioned in these journeys
Senegal Names of natural features
AIR Saharan massifs (generalized)
ATLANTIC OCEAN
MEDITERRANEAN SEA
Tangier
Algiers
Tunis
Tripoli
Alexandria
Cairo
Salā
Fās
Miknāsa
Tilimsān
Marrākush
Sijilmāsa
Canary Islands
Būda
TUWĀT
Taghāzā
HAKKAR
Tāsarahlā
MASSŪFA
AIR
TIBESTI
Iwālātan
Tunbuktū
BARDĀMA
Kawkaw
Takaddā
Zaghari
ZAGHA
Kārsakhū
Niger
Senegal
Bamako
Malli
R Sansara
Niamey
Sokoto
Kano
BARNŪ
L Chad
Chari
YUFI? (Nupe)
Benue
Ibadan
Lagos
Accra
Abijan
Monrovia
Luxor
Uswān
Nile
Aidhab
Judda
Mecca
Mersa Durūr
Sawākin
Dunqala
Khartoum
White Nile
Blue Nile
L Tana
Djibouti
Zaila'
Adan
GULF OF ADEN
AL YAMAN
Zafār al Humūd
Addis Ababa
Bahr el Arab
Ubangi
Congo
L Rudolf
L Albert
Kampala
Nairobi
L Victoria
L Tanganyika
Brazzaville
Luanda
Maqdashaw
Manbasā
Pemba
Zanzibar
Dar es Salaam
Kulwā
INDIAN OCEAN
ATLANTIC OCEAN
Scale of kms. at Equator
Scale of miles at Equator
200 0 1000
200 0 600
18°W 12°W 6°W 0° 6°E 18°E 24°E 30°E 36°E
24°N 18°N 6°N 0° 6°S

of this kind could hardly carry elaborate notes or send home regular reports. Moreover, ibn Baṭṭūṭa underwent such adventures as shipwreck and an armed robbery which left him with only his trousers. The man obviously had a prodigious memory —but the best of memories can deceive, especially where the same place is visited more than once. The old gentleman's narrative was dictated to a scribe who would inevitably make a few mistakes. It was edited by ibn Juzayy, who in his description of his task states that the sultan told ibn Baṭṭūṭa to dictate a description of the places he had seen, of the happenings he remembered, and of the kings, scholars and holy men he had met. The resultant narrative was interesting in itself, gave joy to the reader and hearer as well as being instructive. Ibn Juzayy's task was to put it together in the form of a work which brought out the usefulness of the material, caused it to conform to elegant literary usage, and made it generally suitable for pleasure in reading and edification. Sometimes he had re-expressed ibn Baṭṭūṭa's meaning in his own words but often he had used the traveller's own narrative. He had not attempted to verify anything, for ibn Baṭṭūṭa himself vouches for what he has seen and clearly states what is hearsay. He (ibn Juzayy) had indicated the full pronunciation of strange names and sounds by indicating vowels where necessary.[5]

After ibn Juzayy and the first scribe had finished, the manuscript had to be copied. Luckily there are available at the *Bibliotheque Nationale* in Paris some excellent manuscripts. Indeed, part of one of them may have come from the hands of ibn Juzayy himself. Defrémery and Sanguinetti, the French editors on whose printed text this translation is based, used good manuscripts, but here and there we have had to reject their readings or emendations. We also consulted the Beirut edition but a thoroughly critical text with a full apparatus of variants has still to be produced.

Ibn Juzayy ends his work of editing with the remark: 'It would not be concealed from anybody of sound mind that this shaikh [ibn Baṭṭūṭa] was the traveller of the age, and he who says this man is the [supreme] traveller of this community [Islam] would not be far from the truth'. This tribute remains true six centuries later, and indeed one could say even more in praise of this great man. It is hoped that this work will do a little to make him better known in his own continent which may produce the greatest travellers of coming ages.

It remains to describe briefly how our work came to be written and to give thanks to the many who have helped us. This book originated at Makerere University College at Kampala, Uganda, in 1965. Said Hamdun wanted an Arabic narrative to read with Noel King, for the latter had worked at grammars, handbooks and holy books for years and needed something more flowing and less deadly serious. We settled on ibn Baṭṭūṭa's travels in black Africa, partly because its Arabic is so beautiful, because his narrative is by an African in the big sense of that word and tells us so much about Islam in Africa, and, besides, he was a scholar of Religious Studies. As we went forward it began to seem to Noel King a shame that the running verbal translation by Said Hamdun, himself an African and a Muslim who had studied also in Europe and America, should not reach a wider audience. The text we used for translation was the Arabic of Defrémery and Sanguinetti: *Voyages d'Ibn*

Batoutah, four volumes, Paris, third edition, 1893-1895.[6] The relevant volume number of this work is given in large Roman numerals at the beginning of a passage and the page references are given as they occur within brackets. Noel King copied the consonantal text, Said Hamdun then pointed it and translated it orally. The former transcribed and added notes, many of which were also based on the latter's oral remarks. The work was finished in 1968, but was then overtaken by the misfortunes which collaborative work undergoes when both members are transferred—the one to California in 1968 and the other to Kenya in 1970. In 1973 we returned to the typescript and felt the translation would suffer by total revision, even if we had the time. A great deal has happened in scholarship concerning Africa, especially in Manding studies in these last four years. We cannot claim to be abreast of the experts but we hope the notes, which have been extensively revised, give a true indication of where the action is for those who wish to go into academic detail.

Our debt to the scholars whose writings made our journey so much easier than their own pioneer efforts, ranging from the editors of the text to Sir Hamilton Gibb, is inadequately acknowledged by mentioning their books and articles in the annotated Bibliography. We also thank other scholars for reading through our efforts and making many suggestions and corrections. Dr Humphrey Fisher of the School of Oriental and African Studies at London consistently helped our work in Africa over a period of years: checking out references, revising translations, obtaining photocopies and corresponding faithfully. He and Professor John O. Hunwick looked through the translation and made many helpful suggestions. The Manding and other specialist material was also provided by the latter. Professor W. Montgomery Watt has also given a great deal of help and encouragement. Dr Pierre Cachia, Dr Richard Randolph and Dr Edmund Burke have kindly verified references for us. More recently, Dr Aziz Batran, himself a Sudanese, has gone over our work in detail and assisted in making the notes more up-to-date. For the map we are indebted to Dr David McMaster of the Centre of African Studies and Mr Carson Clarke of the Department of Geography of the University of Edinburgh. Mrs Joan Hodgson of the Inter-Library Loan Desk at the Library at University of California, Santa Cruz, obtained copies of books and manuscripts for us from near and far, giving us such superb service that we did not regret not being able to go in person to Dakar, London, Montreal, Washington, Berkeley and the other places whence she culled our material. The proofs were corrected at Port Moresby and such reference checking as was possible was thanks to the assistance of the Reader Services Staff of the University Library there. We also gratefully thank those who have laboured with the sub-editing, checking of references and typing—Evelyn, Francis and Jeremy King, Alan and Clare Claydon, Mrs Anne Kawuki, Mrs Dot Bergen, Amanda Tanwell and Miss Lilia Osuna.

Mawlid al-Nabī (S.A.W.),
12 Rabī al-awal 1393 A.H.
Palm Sunday, 15 April 1973 A.D.
Nairobi, Kenya and
Santa Cruz, California

SAID HAMDUN
and NOEL KING

NOTES TO INTRODUCTION

[1] *Al-Durar al-Kāmina*, Hyderabad, Andra Pradesh, III, 1929, pp. 480-481.

[2] Ibn Kẖaṭīb was an official of the court at Grenada who died in 1374. The quotation of H. A. R. Gibb is from his Hakluyt edition and translation of *The Travels of Ibn Baṭṭūṭa*. Cambridge, 1958, vol I, p. ix. We shall herafter abbreviate references to this series as 'Gibb: Hakluyt' and give the page and volume number. The Introduction to the whole work is in volume I and the East African section in volume II. The West African section is in volume IV which has not yet been published. Our debt to Gibb is great and we follow his chronology of his Hakluyt series where available, otherwise that of his *Selections* (London, 1929). Sometimes we have accepted the chronological revisions of Ivan Hrbek, 'The Chronology of Ibn Baṭṭūṭa's Travels', *Archiv Orientální*, XXX, 1962, pp. 409-486.

[3] Ibn Marzūq came from Tlemsen in Algeria, held an important post for some years in Cairo and died in 1379. Ibn Juzayy was a scholar who came from Grenada and died in 1356 or 1358. He was clearly an editor and writer of some brilliance and we owe him much, especially for his forbearance with some of the apparently whimsical but inimitable details the traveller gives. The sultan of Morocco was Abū ᶜInān who reigned 1348-1358.

[4] *An Introduction to History*, translated by Franz Rosenthal, Princeton, vol. I, 1958, pp. 369-371.

[5] C. Defrémery et B. R. Sanguinetti, *Voyages d'Ibn Batoutah*, Paris, 1893, vol. I, pp. 9-12; Gibb: Hakluyt, vol. I, pp. 5-7.

[6] The edition of 1854 has been recently reprinted with preface and notes by Vincent Monteil, Paris (the Preface is dated 1968).

THE EAST AFRICAN JOURNEY

ʿAdan, Zailaʿ, Maqdashaw. (Middle or late January, A.D. 1331)

[Ibn Baṭṭūṭa had travelled from his home in Tangier to perform the Pilgrimage. After doing so he stayed at Mecca for two years, then he travelled to Jeddah, was driven by a storm to Ra's al-Dawā'ir and Suakin on the African side of the Red Sea, returned to Arabia, visited Yemen and found his way to ʿAdan [Aden]. There he was able to take a ship sailing to East Africa on the northeast monsoon]

[I 1] In the name of God the merciful, the compassionate . . . [II 179] I travelled from the town of ʿAdan [Aden] by sea for four days and arrived [180] at the city of Zailaʿ [Zeila], the city of the Barbara, who are a people of the blacks; Shāfiʿī by rite.[1] Their country is a desert which extends for a two months' journey, its beginning is at Zailaʿ and its ending is at Maqdashaw [Mogadishu]. Their livestock are camels and their sheep are famed for their fatness. The inhabitants of Zailaʿ are black in colour and the majority are Rejecters [*Rāfiḍi*].[2] It is a big city and has a great market but it is the dirtiest, most desolate and smelliest town in the world. The reason for its stink is the quantity of fish and the blood of the camels they butcher in its alleyways. When we arrived there we preferred to pass the night on the sea, though it was rough. We did not spend the night in the town because of its squalor.

Then we travelled thence by sea for fifteen nights and arrived at Maqdashaw [Mogadishu]. It is a town endless in its size. Its people have many camels [181], of which they slaughter hundreds every day and they have many sheep. Its people are powerful merchants. In it are manufactured the cloths named after it which have no rival, and are transported as far as Egypt and elsewhere.

One of the customs of the people of this city is that when a ship arrives at the anchorage, the *ṣunbūqs* (these are small boats) come out to it. In every *ṣunbūq* is a group of young people of the town, and every one of them brings a covered dish with food in it. He offers it to one of the merchants of the ship and says, 'This is my guest.' Each one of them does similarly. When the merchant disembarks from the ship he goes nowhere but to the house of his host from among these young people. But a man who has frequented the place a good deal and obtained a knowledge of its people may lodge where he wishes. When he lodges with his host, he [the host] sells his goods for him [182] and buys on his behalf. He who buys from him at too low a price or sells to him without the presence of his host—that transaction is considered as rejected.[3] There is profit for them in this custom.

When the young people came to the ship on which I was, one of them came to me. My companions told him, 'This is not a merchant but a *faqīh*'.[4] He shouted to his companions and said to them, 'This is the guest of the *qāḍī*.' One of the *qāḍī*'s people was among them and he informed him of that. The *qāḍi* came to the shore of the sea with a group of students and sent one of them to me. I disembarked with my travelling companions and saluted the *qāḍī* and his company. He said to me, 'In the name of God, let us go to greet the shaikh.' And I said: 'Who is the shaikh?' He said, 'The sultan.' And it is their custom to speak of the sultan as the shaikh. I said to him, 'When I have lodged I will go to him.' He said to me 'It is the custom when a *faqīh* [183] or a *sharīf* or a man of piety comes, that he does not lodge till he has seen the sultan.'[5] I went with them to him as they requested.

AN ACCOUNT OF THE SULTAN OF MAQDASHAW

The sultan of Maqdashaw, as we mentioned, they only call 'the shaikh'. And his name is Abū Bakr son of shaikh ʿUmar. He is in origin from the Barbara, and his speech is Maqdishī, but he knows the Arabic tongue. It is customary when a ship arrives for the sultan's *ṣunbūq* to go out to it. Questions are then asked about the ship, whence it comes, who is its owner, who its *rubbān* (that is, the captain), what its cargo and who of merchants and others has come on it. All that is ascertained and made known to the sultan. Then he gives lodging to him who deserves it near his house. When I arrived with the *qāḍī* whom I mentioned—and he is known as ibn al-Burhān, an Egyptian [184] by origin[6]—at the house of the sultan, one of the young men came out and greeted the *qāḍī* who said to him, 'Take this message with which you are entrusted and let *mawlānā*[7] [our master] the shaikh know that this man has come from the land of al-Ḥijāz [in Arabia].' He did so, then returned bringing with him a dish with some betel leaves and areca nuts on it.[8] He gave me ten leaves and a small quantity of nuts. He gave similarly to the *qāḍī* and what remained on the dish to my travelling companions and the students of the *qāḍī*. And he brought a sprinkler of Damascene rose water which he sprinkled over me and the *qāḍī*.[9] And he said, '*Mawlānā* commands that he lodge in the Scholars' House.' (This is the house prepared for students of Religious Studies.) The *qāḍī* took my hand and we came to that house which is near the shaikh's house. And it was bedded out and set up with what is necessary. Then he came with food from the shaikh's house. With him was one of his *wazīrs* who was in charge of guests.[10] He said, '*Mawlānā* gives you *al-salāmu ʿalaikum* and he says to you, you are most welcome.' Then he put down [185] the food and we ate. Their food is rice cooked with ghee placed on a large wooden dish.[11] They put on top dishes of *kūshān*—this is the relish, of chicken and meat and fish and vegetables. They cook banana before it is ripe in fresh milk and they put it on a dish, and they put sour milk in a dish with pickled lemon on it and bunches of pickled chillies, vinegared and salted, and green ginger and mangoes.[12] These are like apples but they have a stone, and when they ripen they are very sweet and are eaten like fruit. But before they ripen they are bitter like lemons and they pickle them in vinegar. When they eat a ball of rice, they eat after it something from these salted and vinegared foods. Now one of the people of Maqdashaw habitually eats as much as a group of us would. [186] They are extremely large and fat of body. Then when we had eaten, the *qāḍī* left us.

We stayed three days and food was brought to us thrice a day, for that is their custom. When it was the fourth day, a Friday, the *qāḍī* and the students and one of the *wazīrs* of the shaikh came to me. They brought me a suit of their clothing—a silk wrapper to tie around the middle instead of trousers (which they do not know), an upper garment of Egyptian linen with markings, a lined gown of Jerusalem material, and an Egyptian turban with embroideries. They also brought garments for my companions befitting their circumstances. We went to the grand mosque and prayed behind the *maqṣūra*.[13] When the shaikh came out of the gate of the *maqṣūra*, I greeted him together with the *qāḍī*. He welcomed me and spoke in their language to the *qāḍī*. Then he said in the Arabic language, 'You are most welcome. [187] You have honoured our country and given us pleasure.'

He came out to the courtyard of the mosque. He stopped at the grave of his father who was buried there. He read [from the Qur'ān] and prayed. Then the *wazīrs*, the *amīrs*, and the commanders of the soldiers came and greeted him. Their custom in greeting is like the custom of the people of the Yaman. A man puts his index finger on the ground, then raises it to his head, saying: 'May God prolong your might.' Then the shaikh came out of the gate of the mosque, put on his sandals and ordered the *qāḍī* to put on his sandals and me to do the same. He turned to walk towards his house which is near the mosque. All of the people walked barefoot, and there were raised over his head four canopies of coloured silk and on the top of each canopy was the figure of a bird in gold. His clothes that day were a robe of green Jerusalem stuff and underneath it fine loose robes of Eygpt.[14] He was dressed with a wrapper [188] of silk and turbanned with a large turban. Before him drums and trumpets and pipes were played, the *amīrs* of the soldiers were before and behind him, and the *qāḍī*, the *faqīhs*, the *sharīfs* were with him. He entered his council room; in that order, the *wazīrs*, *amīrs* and the commanders of the soldiers sat down there in the audience chamber. A mat was spread out for the *qāḍī* on which nobody may sit with him; the *faqīhs* and *sharīfs* were by him. They continued in this manner till the afternoon prayer, and when they had prayed the *ʿasr* [the late afternoon prayer] with the shaikh, all the soldiers came and stood in lines in accordance with their ranks. Then the drums, pipes, trumpets and the flutes were played. When these are sounded no one moves nor does he shift his position; he who is walking stops and does not move either forward or backward. When they finish beating the drums they greet with their fingers as we have described [189] and go out. That is a custom of theirs every Friday.

When it is Saturday the people come to the door of the shaikh and they sit in covered halls outside the house. The *qāḍī*, the *faqīhs*, the *sharīfs*, the men of piety, the shaikhs and the men who have performed the pilgrimage enter the second council room. They sit on wooden platforms prepared for the purpose. The *qāḍī* is on a platform by himself and each group on a platform reserved for them which nobody shares with them. Then the shaikh sits in his council and sends for the *qāḍī* who sits on his left. Then enter the *faqīhs* and their leaders sit in front of him while the rest of them salute and go away. Then the *sharīfs* enter, their leaders sit before him, the rest of them salute and go away. If they are guests, they sit on his right. Then enter the shaikhs and those who have performed the pilgrimage, and their great ones sit and the rest salute and go away. Then enter [190] the *wazīrs* and *amīrs*; the heads of the soldiers, rank upon rank, they salute and go. Food is brought and the *qāḍī*, the *sharīfs* and whoever is sitting in that session eat with the shaikh and the shaikh eats with them. If he wishes to honour one of the leaders of his *amīrs*, he sends for him that he should eat with them. The rest of the people eat in the dining hall and their eating is according to precedence in the manner of their entrance before the shaikh. Then the shaikh goes into his house and the *qāḍī*, the *wazīrs*, the private secretary, and four of the leading *amīrs* sit for hearing litigation between the members of the public and hearing the cases of people with complaints. In a matter connected with the rules of the *sharīʿa* [religious law] the *qāḍī* passes judgement; in a matter other than that, the members of the council pass judgement, that is, the ministers and the *amīrs*.[15] In a matter where there is need of consultation with the sultan, they write about it to him and he sends out the reply to them immediately on the back of the note [191] in accordance with his view. And such is always their custom.

Then I sailed from the city of Maqdashaw going towards the land of the *Sawāḥil* [coasts], intending to go to the city of Kulwā [Kilwa] which is one of the cities of the land of the Zunūj.[16]

We arrived at the island of Manbasā (and the manner of writing its name is: the 'm' has an 'a', the 'n' is without a vowel, the 'b' has one dot and a short vowel 'a', the 's' is without dots and with a short vowel 'a' and a 'y' [which acts as a terminal 'a']).[17] Manbasā [Mombasa] is a large island with two days' journey by sea between it and the land of the *Sawāḥil*. It has no mainland. Its trees are the banana, the lemon, and the citron. They have fruit which they call the *jammūn*, which is similar to the olive and its stone is like its stone except that it is extremely sweet.[18] There is no cultivation of grain among the people of this island: food is brought to them from the *Sawāhil.* The greater part of their food is bananas and fish. They are Shāfiʿī by rite, they are a religious people, trustworthy and righteous. Their mosques are made of wood, expertly built. At every door [192] of the mosques there are one or two wells. The depth of their wells is a cubit or two. They take water from them in a wooden container into which a thin stick of a cubit's length has been fixed. The ground around the well and the mosque is level. He who wants to enter the mosque washes his feet and enters. There is at its gate a piece of thick matting upon which he rubs his two feet. He who wants to make the ablution holds the pot between his thighs and pours water upon his hands and carries out the ablutions. All the people walk barefoot. We spent the night on this island and travelled by sea to the city of Kulwā [Kilwa].[19] [Kulwa is] a great coastal city. Most of its people are Zunūj, extremely black. They have cuttings on their faces like those on the faces of the Līmiyyīn of Janāda.[20] One of the merchants told me that the city of Sufāla [Sofala] is half a month's journey from the city of Kulwā and that between [193] Sufāla and Yūfī in the land of the Līmiyyīn is a month's journey and from Yūfī gold dust is brought to Sufāla. The city of Kulwā is amongst the most beautiful of cities and most elegantly built. All of it is of wood, and the ceiling of its houses are of *al-dīs* [reeds]. The rains there are great. They are a people devoted to the Holy War because they are on one continuous mainland with unbelieving Zunūj. Their uppermost virtue is religion and righteousness and they are Shāfiʿī in rite.

RUINS OF KILWA

DESCRIPTION OF THE SULTAN OF KULWĀ

Its sultan at the time of my entry into Kulwā was Abū al-Muẓaffar Ḥasan whose *kunya* was Abū al-Mawāhib [father of gifts] because of his many gifts and deeds of generosity.[21] He was much given to razzias upon the land of the Zunūj; he raided them and captured booty. He used to set aside one fifth of it, which he spent in the ways indicated in the book of God the Exalted. He put the share of the kindred [of the prophet, the *sharīfs*] in a treasury by itself. When the *sharīfs* came to him [194] he gave it to them. The *sharīfs* used to come to him from ʿIrāq and Ḥijāz and other places. I saw at his place a group of the *sharīfs* of Ḥijāz, amongst them Muḥammad bin Jammāz, Manṣūr bin Lubaida bin Abū Numayy and Muḥammad bin Shumaila bin Abū Numayy, and I met at Maqdāshaw Tabl bin Kubaish bin Jammāz who was intending to come to him. This sultan is a very humble man. He sits with the poor people [*faqīrs*] and eats with them, and gives respect to people of religion and of prophetic descent.

A STORY CONCERNING THE SULTAN OF KULWĀ'S DEEDS OF GENEROSITY

I was present with him on a Friday when he came out from the prayer and was returning to his house. He was confronted on the road by one of the Yemeni *faqīrs*. He said to him, 'O father of gifts.' He replied, 'At your service, O *faqīr*, what is your need?' He said, 'Give me these clothes which you are wearing.' He replied, 'Yes, I will give them to you.' He said to him, 'This very moment.' He said, 'Yes, this very moment.' He went back to the mosque and went into the house of the preacher [*khatīb*]. He put on other clothes and took off those [195] clothes. He said to the *faqīr*, 'Enter and take them.' So the *faqīr* went in, tied them in a piece of cloth and put them on his head and went away. The gratitude of the people to the sultan increased at the evidence of his humility and graciousness. His son and heir-apparent took that suit of clothes from the *faqīr* and compensated him for it with ten slaves. When the news reached the sultan of the gratitude of the people to him for that deed he ordered the *faqīr* to be given in addition ten head of fine slaves and two loads of ivory. (The greater part of their gifts are ivory and seldom do they give gold.) When this honourable and generous sultan was gathered to God (may God have mercy on him), his brother Dā'ūd succeeded him. He was the opposite from him. When a beggar came to him he said to him, 'He who used to give has died, and he did not leave anything after him to be given.' The visitors would stay at his house many months and then he would give them a little, until visitors stopped coming to his door. We went by sea from Kulwā to the city of Ẓafār al Ḥumūḍ which is at the end of the land of the Yaman [in Arabia].[22]

THE WEST AFRICAN JOURNEY

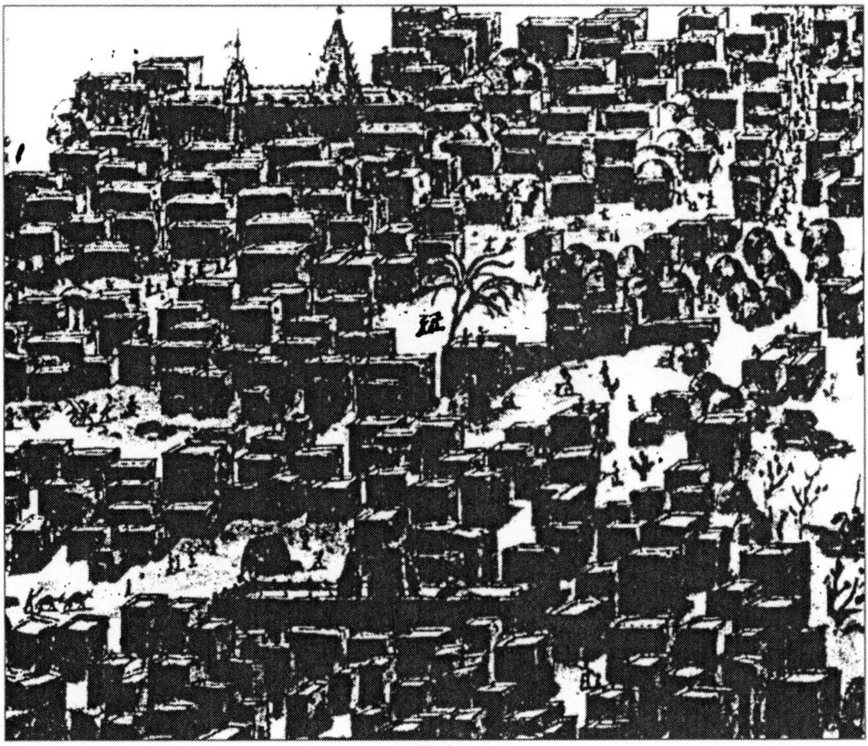

TIMBUKTU
(Drawing by René Caillé in 1878)

IBN BAṬṬŪṬA'S LAST JOURNEY—MOROCCO ACROSS THE SAHARA TO WEST AFRICA AND BACK[23] (753 A.H., 1352 A.D. TO 754/1353)

[Ibn Baṭṭūṭa's visit to East Africa was carried out when he was still a young man. After many adventures in central Asia, India, the Maldive Islands and as far afield as China, he returned home to Tangier. Even so he could not sit still and went to visit Spain. Then he returned home but could not resist the lure of the most terrible journey of all—across the desert to the land of the blacks.]

[IV 376] A RESUMPTION . . .

I travelled from Marrākus͟h in the company of the exalted caravan of our Lord [the sultan of Morocco] (may God support him) and we arrived at the city of Salā, then at the city of Miknāsa, the wonderful, the green, the many-flowered, which has gardens and orchards surrounding it and is in a sea of plantations of olive trees in all directions. Then we arrived at the capital Fās [Fez] (may God Most High protect her!) There I took leave from our Lord (may God give him support!) and I left in my travelling clothes for the land of the blacks [bilād as-Sūdān]. I arrived at the town of Sijilmāsa. It is a lovely city. In it there are a great deal of sweet dates. The town of Baṣra is like it for the abundance of its dates, but the dates of Sijilmāsa are sweeter.

The kind of date called *irār* has no like anywhere. I stayed there with the *faqīh* Abū Muḥammad al Bushrī [377]—he whose brother I met in the town of Qanjanfū [Kuang-chou near Canton?] in the land of China. How far apart they are! He was generous to the extreme. And I bought camels there and their fodder for four months.

Then I travelled at the beginning of the month of God, Muḥarram, in the year 'fifty-three [753 A.H., 18 February A.D. 1352] with travel companions whose leader was Abū Muhammad Yandakān al-Massūfī, may God have mercy on him. In the company was a group of the merchants of Sijilmāsa and others. We arrived after twenty-five days at Taghāzā. It is a village with no good in it. Amongst its curiosities is the fact that the construction of its houses and its mosques is of rock salt with camel skin roofing and there are no trees in it, the soil is just sand. In it is a salt mine. It is dug out of the ground and is found there in huge slabs, one on top of another as if it had been carved [378] and put under the ground. A camel can carry two slabs of salt. Nobody lives in it except slaves of the Massūfa who dig for the salt and live on dates brought to them from Darᶜa and Sijilmāsa, and on the meat of camels, and on *anlī* which is brought from the land of the blacks.[24] The blacks arrive from their country and carry away the salt from there. A camel load of it is sold in Īwālātan [Walata] for from eight to ten *mithqāls*, and in the town of Māllī for twenty to thirty *mithqāls*, perhaps the price reaches up to forty.[25] The blacks exchange the salt as money as one would exchange gold and silver. They cut it up and trade with it in pieces. In spite of the insignificance of the village of Taghāzā, the trading in it comes to the equivalent of many *qinṭars* of gold dust. We stayed in it ten days in miserable condition [379], because its water is bitter andit is of all places the most full of flies. In it water is drawn for the entry into the desert which comes after it. This desert is a travelling distance of ten days and there is no water in it except rarely.[26] But we found much water in it in pools left behind by the rains. One day we found a pool of sweet water between two hillocks of rocks. We quenched our thirst from it and washed our clothes. In that desert truffles are abundant. There are also so many lice in it that people put strings around their necks in which there is mercury which kills the lice. In those days we used to go ahead in front of the caravan. When we found a place suitable for pasture we would let the animals pasture. We did not cease from that practice until a man known as ibn Zīrī was lost in the desert. I did not go ahead after that [380] nor stay behind.

Ibn Zīrī had a quarrel and altercation with the son of his maternal uncle who was called ibn ʿAdī and he stayed behind the company and lost his way. When people dismounted there was no news of him. I advised his cousin to hire someone from the Massūfa to follow his tracks so that he might perhaps find him. He refused. The day after, a man of the Massūfa without payment volunteered to seek him and found his tracks. He had followed the beaten track, sometimes going out of it and sometimes not. He did not find him nor news of him. We met a caravan on the way. They informed us that some men had stayed behind. We found one of them dead under a little tree of the kind that grows in the sand. His clothes were on him and a whip was in his hand. The water was about a mile from him.

Then [381] we arrived at Tāsarahlā where water is exuded by

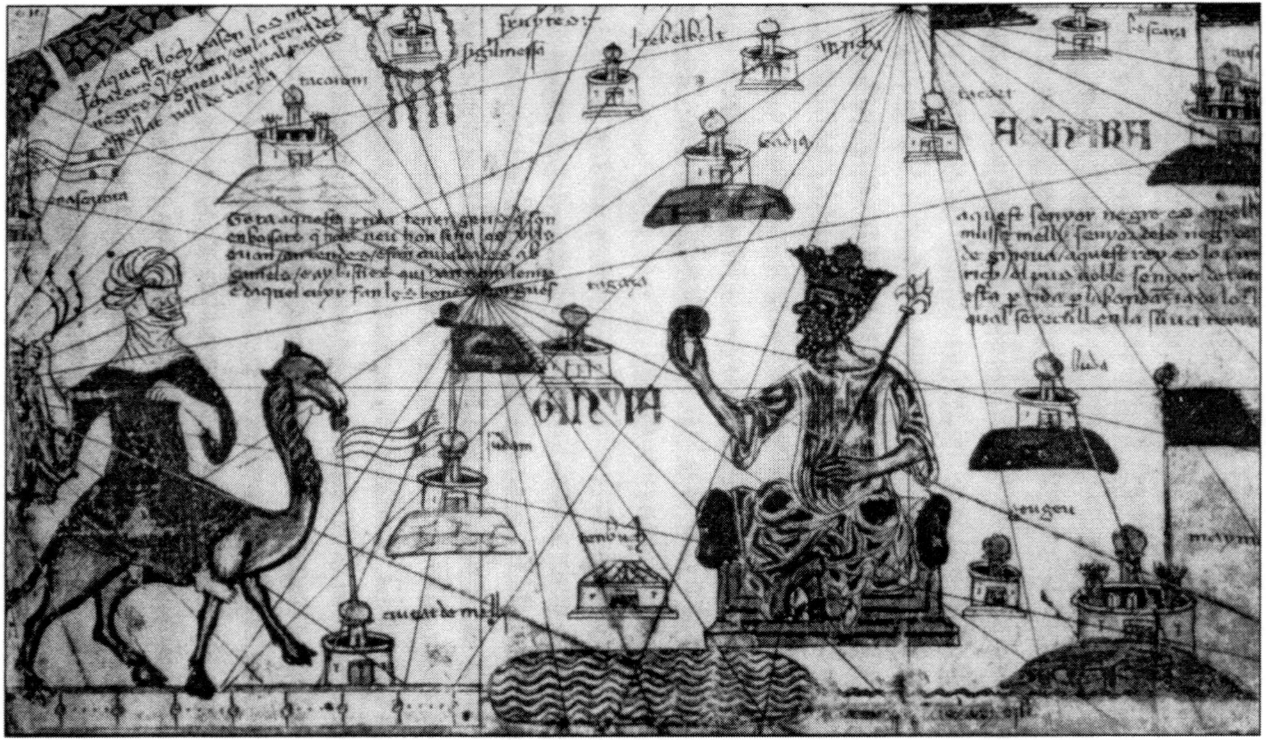

A PANEL OF THE CATALAN MAP
(Drawn by Abraham Cresques in 1375)

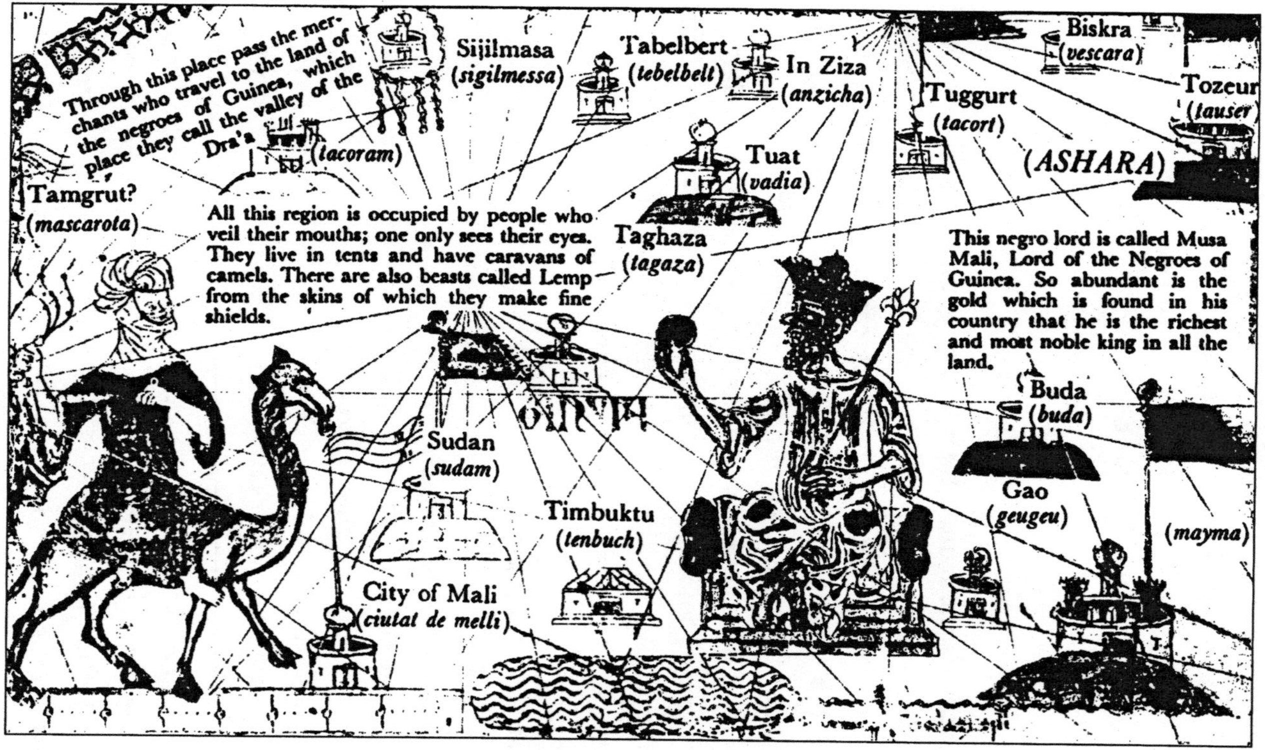

KEY TO THE CATALAN MAP

the ground. The caravans dismount there and stay three days. They rest and repair their water-bags and fill them with water. They stitch covers on them as a protection from the wind. From there the *takshīf* is sent.[27]

AN ACCOUNT OF THE TAKSHĪF

The *takshīf* is the name given to every man of the Massūfa who is hired by the people of the caravan to go ahead to Īwālātan with the letters of the people to their friends there, so as to rent houses for them and to come out to meet them with water a distance of four days. He who has no friend in Īwālātan writes to a person who is known among the merchants of Īwālātan for his generosity and he enters into partnership with him. If perhaps the *takshīf* perishes [382] in this desert, then the people of Īwālātan do not know about the caravan, so its people, or most of them, perish.

That desert has many devils, and if the *takshīf* be alone, they play with him and lure him on until he loses his way and perishes since there is no way which is clear there and no tracks. There is only sand blown by the wind. You see mountains of sand in a place, then you see they have moved to another. The guide there is a person who has frequented that route and has intelligence. I saw as a remarkable thing that the man who was our guide was blind in one eye and sick in the second. But he was the most knowledgeable of people with regard to the road. We hired the *takshīf* on this journey for one hundred *mithqāls* of gold. He was of the Massūfa. On the night of the seventh day we saw the fires of those [383] who came out for our meeting and we were happy about that. This desert is bright, full of sunlight, one's chest is dilated, the soul finds good in it, it is secure from robbers. There are many wild cattle, a herd of them can come so near to people that they can hunt them with dogs and arrows. But their meat when eaten generates a thirst. Many people avoid it because of that. A curious thing about these cattle is that when they are killed water is found in their stomach. I have seen people of the Massūfa pressing the stomach of one of them and drinking the water in it. There are also many serpents in this desert.

AN ANECDOTE

There was in the caravan a merchant of Tilimsān [Tlemcen], known as al Ḥājj Zayyān. It was his custom to seize snakes and play with them. I used to tell him not to [384], but he did not desist. So on another day he put his hand on the hole of a lizard to bring it out. He found in its place a snake. He took hold of it with his hand. He wanted to mount and it bit him on the index finger of the right hand. He was affected by great pain. His hand was cauterized but the pain increased later in the day. He killed a camel and put his hand in its stomach and left it like that all night. Then the flesh of his finger came off and he cut it off at the base. People of the Massūfa told us that that snake must have had a drink of water before biting him; if it had not drunk, it would have killed him.

When those who had come out to meet us arrived with the water, we gave our horses drink and we entered a desert of intense heat, not like the one we were accustomed to. We used to set out after the later afternoon prayer and travel all night, dismounting [385] in the morning. Men from the Massūfa and Bardāma and others would come with loads of water for sale. Then we arrived at the town of Īwālātan [Walata] at the beginning of the month of Rabiᶜi al'Awwal after a journey of two whole months from Sijilmāsa. It is the first district of the blacks, and the representative of the sultan in it was Farbā Ḥusain, and the meaning of 'Farbā' is 'the representative'. And when we arrived there, the merchants placed their goods in an open place and the blacks undertook to look after them. They went to the Farba. He was sitting on a mat in a roofed open hall and his helpers were before him with spears and bows in their hands and the elders of the Massūfa behind him. The merchants stood in front of him and he spoke to them through an interpreter in spite of their nearness to him, in derision of them. At that moment I regretted my arrival in their country because of the badness [386] of their manners and their despising of the whites.[28]

I went to the house of ibn Baddāᶜ, an excellent man of the people of Salā. I had written to him to rent a house for me and he had done that. Then the Overseer of Īwālātan, whose name was Manshā Jū, invited those who had come in the caravan to his hospitality. I refused to attend that affair, but my friends insisted very much; so I went with the rest. Then the meal was brought out: a concoction of *anlī* mixed with a drop of honey and milk, which they placed in a half calabash like a deep wooden bowl. Those present drank and went away. I said to them, 'Was it for this the black invited us?' They said, 'Yes, this is great entertainment in their country.'[29] I became sure then that there was no good to be expected from them. I wanted to travel back with the pilgrims of Īwālātan. [387] Then it seemed good to me to go to see the capital [or: residence, presence] of their King. My residence in Īwālātan was about fifty days. Its people were generous to me and entertained me. Among my hosts was its *qāḍī*, Muḥammad ibn ʿAbd Allāh ibn Yanūmar and his brother, the *faqīh* and teacher Yaḥyā. The town of Īwālātan is very hot and there are in it a few small date palms in whose shade they plant melons. They obtain water from the ground which exudes it. Mutton is obtainable in quantity there. The clothes of its people are of fine Egyptian material. Most of the inhabitants belong to the Massūfa, and as for their women—they are extremely beautiful and are more important than the men.

ANECDOTE CONCERNING THE MASSŪFA WHO INHABIT ĪWĀLĀTAN

The condition of these people [388] is strange and their manners outlandish. As for their men, there is no sexual jealousy in them. And none of them derives his genealogy from his father but, on the contrary, from his maternal uncle. A man does not pass on inheritance except to the sons of his sister to the exclusion of his own sons. Now that is a thing I never saw in any part of the world except in the country of the unbelievers of the land of Mulaībār [Malabar] among the Indians. As to the former [the Massūfa], they are Muslims keeping to the prayers, studying *fiqh* [islamic jurisprudence], and learning the Qur'ān by heart. With regard to their women, they are not modest in the presence of men, they do not veil themselves in spite of their perseverance in the prayers.[30] He who wishes to marry among them can marry, but the women do not travel with the husband, and if one of them wanted to do that, she would be prevented by her family. The women there have friends and companions amongst men outside the prohibited degrees of marriage [i.e., other than brothers, fathers, etc.]. Likewise for the men, [389] there are companions from amongst women outside the prohibited degrees. One of them would enter his house to find his wife with her companion and would not disapprove of that conduct.

ANECDOTE

One day I entered upon the *qāḍī* in Īwālātan after he had given his permission for me to enter. I found with him a woman—young in age and very beautiful. When I saw her, I was taken aback and wanted to retrace my steps. She laughed at me and was not overcome by modesty. The *qāḍī* said to me, 'Why are you retreating? She is only my companion.' I was astonished at their conduct—for he was from the *faqīh* class and had performed the pilgrimage. I was informed that he had asked permission of the sultan to go on the pilgrimage that year with his female companion—I do not know whether she was this one or not—anyhow, the sultan did not permit him.

[390] AN ANECDOTE LIKE IT

One day I entered upon Abū Muḥammad Yandakān, a man of the Massūfa, the one in whose company we had arrived. I found him sitting on a mat and in the middle of his house was a bed with a canopy. On it was a woman and with her a man was sitting, and the two were conversing. I said to him, 'Who is this woman?' He said, 'She is my wife.' I said, 'What is [the relationship of] the man with her to her?' He said, 'He is her companion.' I said, 'Do you accept this when you have lived in our country and have known the matters of the *sharᶜ* [divine law]?' He said to me, 'Women's companionship with men in our country is honourable and takes place in a good way: there is no suspicion about it. They are not like the women in your country.' I was astonished at his thoughtless answer and I went away from him and did not go to him after this. Though he invited me many times, I did not respond.

When I decided on the journey [391] to Malli which is twenty-four days of travel from Īwālātan for a person who exerts himself, I hired a guide from the Massūfa, since there is no need to travel with companions because of the safety of that road, and went out with three of my friends.[31] That road has many trees which are tall and of great girth: a caravan can find shade in the shadow of one tree; some of them have no branches and no leaves, but the shadow of its trunk is such that a man can find shade in it. Some of those trees have rotted inside and rainwater collects in them. Such a tree is like a well and people drink of the water which is in it. Bees and honey are in some and people extract the honey from the trees. I have passed by one of these trees and found inside it a weaver with his loom set up in it—he was weaving. I was amazed by him. Ibn Juzayy says that in the land of al-Andalus there are two trees of the chestnut type [392] in the hollow trunk of each one of which a weaver weaves clothes. One of them was in the side of the valley of Āsh [Guadix], the other at Bushshāra [Alpuxaras] in Grenada.[32] To resume—in the trees of this forest which is between Īwālātan and Malli, there are trees whose fruits are like those of plums, apples, peaches and apricots, though they are not quite the same as these. There are trees that bear fruit like the cucumber, when it ripens it bursts uncovering something like flour: they cook it and eat it and it is sold in the markets.[33] They dig out from the ground a crop like beans and they fry and eat it. Its taste is like fried peas. Sometimes they grind it and make from it something like a sponge cake, frying it with *gharti*: *gharti* is a fruit like a plum which is very sweet and harmful to white men when they eat it. The hard part inside is crushed and an oil is extracted from it. From this they derive [393] a number of benefits. Amongst these are: they cook with it, fuel the lamps, fry that sponge I mentioned with it, they use it as an ointment, and they mix it with a kind of earth of theirs and plaster the houses with it in the way whitewash is used. Amongst them it is plentiful and easy to come by, and it is carried from one town to another in big calabashes.[34] One of the calabashes is big enough to contain what a large jar would contain in our country. The calabashes in the land of the blacks become big and from them they make wooden dishes. They cut the calabash in two halves and make from it two dishes and they decorate them with beautiful decorations. When one of them travels he is followed by his men and women slaves carrying his bedding and the vessels from which he eats and drinks which are made out of calabashes. The traveller in this land carries neither food nor relishes and no *dīnārs* or *dirhams* [i.e., coins large or small in value]. He only carries [394] slabs of salt and glass trinkets which the people call beads and some perfumery. The things which please them most are cloves, aromatic gums, and *tāsirghant*, which is their incense. When the traveller arrives in a village the women of the blacks come with *anlī* and milk and chickens and flour of *nabaq* [lotus], rice, and *fūnī* [fonio), this is like the grain of mustard and from it *kuskusu* and porridge are made, and bean flour.[35] He buys from them what he likes, but not rice, as eating the rice is harmful to white men and the *fūnī* is better than it.

After a distance of ten days' travel from Īwālātan, we arrived at the village of Zāgharī, which is a big place with black merchants living in it. They are called Wanjarāta, and there live with them a group of white men who follow the sect [395] of the Ibādī from amongst the Kh̲ārijites. They are called Ṣag̲ha-nag̲hū.[36] The Sunni *mālikī* among the white men in that country are called Tūrī.[37] From this town *anlī* is brought to Īwālātan. Then we went from Zāg̲harī and arrived at the great river, the Nile. On it is the town of Kārsak̲h̲ū. The Nile descends from it to Kābara, then to Zāg̲ha.[38] Kābara and Zāg̲ha have two sultans who give obedience to the king of Malli. And the people of Zāg̲ha are old in Islam, they are religious and seekers after knowledge.

Then the Nile comes down from Zāg̲ha to Tunbuktū (Timbuktu], then to Kawkaw [Gao], the two places we shall mention below. Then it comes to the town of Mūlī, which is the land of the Līmiyyūn and is the last county of Malli. Then the river flows to Yūfī [Nupe?], which is one of the biggest cities of [396] the blacks. Their sultan is one of their greatest sultans. A white

RUINS OF WALATA

man cannot go there because they would kill him before he arrived there. Then the river comes down from there to the land of the Nubians who follow the Naṣrāniyya [Christian] faith, and on to Dunqula [Dongola], which is the biggest town in their land. Their sultan is called ibn Kanz al-Dīn who became Muslim in the days of al-Malik al-Nāṣir. Then it descends to the cataracts. This is the last district of the blacks and the first of Uswān [Aswan] in Upper Egypt.[39]

I saw a crocodile in this place [i.e., at Kārshkhū] on the Nile near the shore like a small canoe. One day I went down to the Nile to answer a need and one of the blacks came and stood between me and the river. I was astonished at his bad manners and the paucity of his shame. I mentioned that to some one. He answered, 'He only did that for fear on your behalf of danger from the crocodile [397]. He made a barrier between you and it.'

Then we went from Kārsakhū and reached a river called the Ṣanṣara, which is about ten miles from Malli.[40] It is their custom to prevent people entering the city except with permission. I had written beforehand to the white community whose leaders are Muḥammad ibn al-Faqīh al-Juzūlī and Shams al-Din ibn al Naqwīsh, the Egyptian, to rent me a house.

When I arrived at the river just mentioned, I crossed in a ferry and nobody prevented me. I arrived at the city of Malli, the capital of the king of the blacks. I alighted by the graveyard and went to the quarter of the whites. I sought out Muḥammad ibn al-Faqīh and found he had rented a house for me opposite his own. I went to it and his son-in-law, the *faqīh* and the Qur'ān reciter, ʿAbd al-Wāḥid, came with candles and food. Then [398] on the following day there came to me ibn al-Faqīh,

Shams al-Dīn ibn al-Naqwīsh and ʿAli al-Zūdī al-Marrākushī (he is a scholar). I met the *qāḍī* of Malli, ʿAbd al-Rahmān, who came to see me: he is a black, has been on the pilgrimage, and is a noble person with good qualities of character. He sent me a cow as his hospitality gift. I met the interpreter Dūgẖā, a noble black and a leader of theirs. He sent me a bull. The *faqīh* ʿAbd al-Wāḥid sent me two sacks of *fūnī* and a calabash of *gharti*. Ibn al-Faqīh sent me rice and *fūnī*. Shams al-Din sent me a hospitality gift. They performed their duty towards me [as a guest] most perfectly; may God bless and reward them for their good deeds! Ibn al-Faqīh was married to the daughter of the paternal uncle of the sultan and she used to take care of us with food and other things.

Ten days after our arrival we ate [399] a porridge made from a thing like colocasia called *qāfī*, to them it is preferable over the rest of the food. The following morning we all became ill. We were six in number and one died. I went to Morning Prayer and fainted during it. I asked one of the Egyptians for a laxative medicine. He brought something called *baidar*, made of plant roots, mixed it with aniseed and sugar and beat it up in water. I drank it and vomited up what I had eaten with a lot of bile. And God preserved me from destruction, but I was sick for two months.

AN ACCOUNT OF THE SULTAN OF MALLI, MANSĀ SULAIMĀN[41]

The sultan of Malli is sultan Mansā Sulaimān: 'Mansā' means 'sultan', and Sulaimān is his name. He is a miserly king, not much giving is to be expected from him. It happened [400] that I stayed this period and did not see him because of my sickness. Then he made food on the occasion of the period of mourning for our Lord Abū'l'Ḥasan (may God be pleased with him!).[42] He invited the *amīrs* and *faqīhs* and the *qāḍī* and the *khatīb* [preacher], and I attended with them. They brought reading stools and the Qur'ān was read through completely. They prayed for our Lord Abū'l Ḥasan (may God have mercy on him), and for Mansā Sulaimān. When they had finished this I came forward and greeted Mansā Sulaimān. The *qāḍī* and the preacher and ibn al-Faqīh told him about my condition. He answered in their tongue and they said to me, 'The sultan says to you "Thank God".' I said, 'Praise to God and thanks in every situation.'

ANECDOTE CONCERNING THEIR INSIGNIFICANT HOSPITALITY AND THEIR OSTENTATION CONCERNING IT

When I went [back to my lodgings] a hospitality gift was sent to me and it was directed to the house of the *qāḍī*. He sent it [401] with his men to the house of ibn al-Faqīh. The latter came out from his house in a hurry with bare feet. He entered my house and said, 'Stand up, the sultan's stuff and his present have come for you.' I stood up, thinking they were robes of honour and things of value. But behold—they were three circular pieces of bread, a piece of beef fried in *gharti*, and a calabash of sour milk. When I saw them, I laughed and wondered a lot at their weakness of mind and their magnifying of the insignificant.

ACCOUNT OF MY SPEAKING TO THE SULTAN AFTER THAT AND HIS KINDNESS TO ME

I stayed after the sending of this hospitality gift two months, during which nothing reached me from the sultan. Then came the month of Ramaḍān. Meanwhile I had been going frequently to [402] the place of audience [*mashwar*], greeting him and sitting with the *qāḍī* and the preacher. I had a word with Dūghā, the interpreter. He said, 'Speak before him and I will express on your behalf what is necessary.' At a session at the beginning of Ramaḍān, I stood before the sultan and said to him, 'I have indeed travelled in the lands of the world. I have met their kings. I have been in your country four months and you have given me no hospitality and have not given me anything. What shall I say about you before the sultans?' He said, 'Indeed, I have not seen you nor did I know about you.' The *qāḍī* and ibn al-Fāqīh got up and answered him saying, 'He has greeted you and you sent him food.' Then the sultan ordered a house for me in which I stayed and he fixed an allowance for me. Then he shared out money among the *qāḍī*, the preacher and the men of *fiqh* on the night of the twenty-seventh of Ramaḍān. They call it the *zakāt*.[43] He gave me a share with them of thirty-three and a third *mithqāls*. He was gracious to me at my departure, to the extent of giving me one hundred *mithqāls* of gold.

[403] AN ACCOUNT OF THE SULTAN'S SITTING IN HIS CUPOLA

The sultan has a raised cupola which is entered from inside his house. He sits in it a great part of the time. It has on the audience side a chamber with three wooden arches, the woodwork is covered with sheets of beaten silver and beneath these, three more covered with beaten gold, or, rather, it is silver covered with gilt. The windows have woollen curtains which are raised on a day when the sultan will be in session in his cupola: thus it is known that he is holding a session. When he sits, a silken cord is put out from the grill of one of the arches with a scarf of Egyptian embroidery tied to it. When the people see the scarf, drums are beaten and bugles sounded. Then from the door of the palace come out about three hundred slaves. Some have bows in their hands and some small spears and shields. Some of the spearmen stand on the right and some on the left, the bowmen sit [404] likewise. Then they bring two mares saddled and bridled, and with them two rams. They say that these are effective against the evil eye. When the sultan has sat down three of his slaves go out quickly to call his deputy, Qanjā Mūsā. The *farāriyya* [commanders] arrive, and they are the *amīrs* [officers], and among them are the preacher and the men of *fiqh*, who sit in front of the armed men on the right and left of the place of audience. The interpreter Dūghā stands at the door of the audience chamber wearing splendid robes of *zardkhāna* and others.[44] On his head is a turban which has fringes, they have a superb way of tying a turban. He is girt with a sword whose sheath is of gold, on his feet are light boots and spurs. And nobody wears boots that day except he. In his hands there are two small spears, one of gold and one of silver with points of iron. The soldiers, the district governors, the pages and the Massūfa and others are seated [405] outside the place of audience in a broad street which has trees in it.[45] Each *farārī* [commander] has his followers before him with their spears, bows, drums and bugles made of elephant tusks. Their instruments of music are made of reeds and calabashes, and they beat them with sticks and produce a wonderful sound. Each *farārī* has a quiver which he places between his shoulders. He holds his bow in his hand and is mounted on a mare. Some of his men are on foot and some on mounts.

Inside the audience chamber under the arches a man is standing; he who wants to speak to the sultan speaks to Dūg̱hā, Dūg̱hā speaks to the man who is standing, and he speaks to the sultan.

AN ACCOUNT OF THE SESSIONS IN THE PLACE OF AUDIENCE

The sultan sits on certain days in the palace yard to give audience. There is a platform under a tree with three steps which they call *banbī*.[46] [406] It is covered with silk and has pillows placed on it. The *shaṭr* is raised, this is a shelter made of silk with a golden bird like a sparrowhawk above it.[47] The sultan comes out from a gate in the corner of the palace, bow in hand, his quiver between his shoulders, and on his head a cap of gold tied with a golden band which has fringes like thin-bladed knives more than a span long. He often wears a robe which is soft and red, made from Roman cloth called *muṭanfas*.[48] The singers go out before him carrying gold and silver *qanābir*[49] and behind him come three hundred armed slaves. The sultan walks slowly and pauses often and sometimes he stops completely. When he comes to the *banbī* he stops and looks at the people. Then he mounts the steps with dignity in the manner of a preacher getting into the pulpit. [407] When he sits down they beat the drums, blow the bugles and the horns, and three of the slaves go out in haste and call the deputy and the *farāriyya* [commanders]. They enter and sit down. The two mares are brought in with the two rams. Dūghā stands at the door while the rest of the people are in the street under the tree.

AN ACCOUNT OF THE SELF-ABASEMENT OF THE BLACKS BEFORE THEIR KING, THEIR DUSTING THEMSELVES FOR HIM, AND OTHER PECULIAR THINGS

The blacks are the most humble of men before their king and the most extreme in their self-abasement before him. They swear by his name, saying, 'Mansā Sulaimānkī' [the law of Mansā Sulaimān]. When he calls one of them while he is in session in his cupola which we described above, the man invited takes off his clothes and wears patched clothes, takes off his turban, puts on a dirty cap, and goes in [408] raising his clothes and trousers up his legs half-way to his knees. He advances with humility looking like a beggar. He hits the ground with his elbows, he hits it hard. He stands bowed, like one in the *rukuʿ* position in prayer, listening to what the king says. When one of them speaks to the sultan and he gives him an answer, he removes his clothes from his back and throws dust on his head and back, as a person does when bathing with water. I used to wonder how they do not blind their eyes. When the sultan speaks in his council, at his word those present take their turbans off their heads and listen to the speech.

Sometimes one of them would stand before him and recall

what he had done in his service, saying, 'I did such and such on such a day,' and, 'I killed so and so on such a day.' Those who know this confirm that he is telling the truth. Their confirmation is by pulling the strings of their bows and letting them go, as one does when one is shooting. If the sultan says to him that he has spoken the truth [409] or thanks him, he takes off his clothes and dusts. This is good manners among them.

Ibn Juzzayy says:

> I have been informed by a keeper of the seal, the *faqīh*, Abū al-Qāsim, son of Riḍwān (may Allah strengthen him!) that when al-Ḥājj Mūsa the Wanjarātī came as ambassador from Mansā Sulaimān to our lord Abū al-Ḥasan (may Allah be pleased with him!)—when he entered the Noble Assembly, one of his men carried with him a round basket and he dusted every time our lord said a gracious word to him as he would in his own country.[50]

AN ACCOUNT OF WHAT THE SULTAN DOES AT THE ʿID PRAYERS AND THEIR ACCOMPANYING DAYS

I was present at Malli for two festivals—the Feast of Sacrifices and the Feast of Fast-breaking.[51] The people came out to the Place of Prayer which is near the sultan's [410] palace wearing good white clothes. The sultan was riding: he had the *ṭailasān* on his head, and the blacks do not wear the *ṭailasān* except at festivals, although the *qāḍī* and the preacher and the *faqīhs* do indeed wear this headdress on other days.[52] On a festival day they precede the sultan and declare the oneness and greatness of God.[53] Before the sultan are carried red banners made of silk. Near the Place of Prayer a tent has been set up. The sultan goes

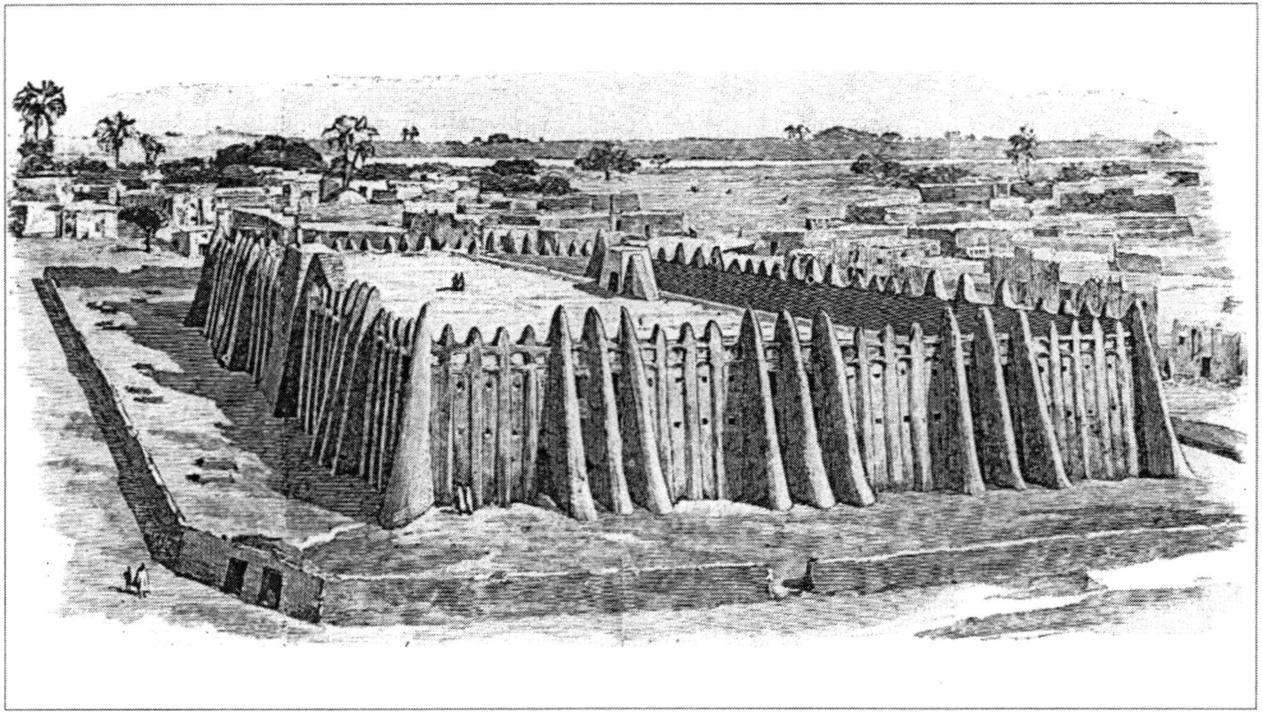

WEST AFRICAN MOSQUE OF THE 14TH CENTURY IN TIMBUKTU

into it, puts himself in order, then he comes out to the Place of Prayer, the prayer is performed and a sermon delivered. The preacher comes down from the pulpit and sits down before the sultan. He makes a long speech. There is there a man with a spear in his hand who explains the things said by the preacher to the people in their tongue. The speech is made up of exhortation, reminders [of the hereafter], praise for the sultan, encouragement to remain obedient, and to give respect as is appropriate.[54]

The sultan holds sessions [411] during the days associated with the two festivals after the *ᶜasr* [late afternoon] prayers on the *banbī*.[55] The men-at-arms come with wonderful weaponry: quivers of silver and gold, swords covered with gold, their sheaths of the same, spears of silver and gold and wands of crystal. Four of the *amīrs* stand behind him to drive off flies, with ornaments of silver in their hands which look like riding stirrups. The *farāriyya* [commanders], the *qāḍī*, and the preacher sit according to custom, the interpreter Dūgh̲ā brings in his four wives and his concubines, who are about a hundred in number. On them are fine clothes and on their heads they have bands of silver and gold with silver and gold apples as pendants. A chair is set there for Dūgh̲a to sit on and he beats an instrument which is made of reeds [412] with tiny calabashes below it, praising the sultan, recalling in his song his expeditions and deeds.[56] The wives and the concubines sing with him and they play with bows. There are with them about thirty of his pages wearing red woollen robes and white caps on their heads. Each one of them has a drum tied to him and he beats it. Then come his retinue of young men who play and turn in the air as they do in Sind. They have a wonderful gracefulness and lightness in this. They juggle with swords beautifully and Dūg͟hā performs a marvellous game with the sword. At that point, the sultan orders that a gift be given him, they bring him a purse of two hundred *mithqāls* of gold dust. An announcement of its contents is made to him over the heads of the people. The *farāriyya* [commanders] get up and twang their bows, thanking the sultan.

On the following day every one of them makes a gift to Dūg͟hā [413] according to his means. Every Friday after the *ʿasr* prayer Dūg͟hā performs ceremonies like those which we have recounted.

AN ACCOUNT OF THE LAUGHABLE MANNER IN WHICH THEIR POETS HOLD A RECITATION

When it is a festival day and Dūg͟hā has completed his play, the poets called the *julā'* (and the singular is *jālī*) come.[57] Each one of them has got inside a costume made of feathers to look like a thrush with a wooden head made for it and a red beak as if it were the head of a bird. They stand before the sultan in that ridiculous attire and recite their poetry. It was mentioned to me that their poetry is a kind of preaching. In it they tell the sultan that this *banbī* on which he is, such and such of the kings of Malli sat on it [414], and such and such were the good deeds of one, and such and such another's. 'So do good, that good will be recounted after you.' Then the Archpoet mounts the steps of the *banbī* and places his head on the sultan's lap. Then he climbs to the top of the *banbī* and places it on his right shoulder, then on the left, meanwhile speaking in their tongue; thereupon he comes down. I was informed that this performance is old amongst them; they continued it from before Islam.

AN ANECDOTE

I was present in the audience of the sultan one day when there came one of their *faqīhs*. He had arrived from a distant district. He stood up before the sultan and spoke many words. The *qāḍī* got up and confirmed his words and the two of them were confirmed by the sultan. Everyone of them took off his turban from his head and dusted before him. There was [415] next to me a man who said to me, 'Do you know what they said?' I said, 'I do not know.' He said:

> 'The *faqīh* reported that locusts fell on their land. One of their pious men went out to the place where the locusts were. He was frightened by their quantity. He said, "This is too great a number of locusts." One of the locusts answered him, "Truly there is too great wrong in the land, God sends us to spoil that which is planted." The *qāḍī* confirmed his statement and so did the sultan. He said to the *amīrs* [officers], "I am innocent of wrong, him who commits wrong amongst you, I shall punish. The man who knows about a wrongdoer and does not inform me about him, the crime of that wrongdoer is upon him, and God will be his reckoner and interrogator." When he uttered this statement, the *farāriyya* [commanders] took off their turbans from their heads and declared their innocence from wrongdoing.[58]

AN ANECDOTE

[416] Another time I was present at the Friday prayers. There stood up one of the merchants from among the scholars of the

Massūfa. His name was Abū Ḥafṣ. He said, 'O people of the mosque, I make you witnesses to the case I have against Mansā Sulaimān before the Apostle of God (may God grant him grace and peace!)' When he said that there came out to him a group of men from the *maqṣūra* [sovereign's enclosure] of the sultan. They asked him, 'Who wronged you, who has taken anything from you?' He said, '*Mansha* Jū of Īwālātan,' that is, the governor, 'he took from me what is valued at six hundred *mithqāls*. He wanted to give me as its value only one hundred *mithqāls*.' The sultan sent for him. As soon as he appeared after some days he sent them both to the *qāḍī* who confirmed the merchant's right and he took the award. After that the governor was removed from his work.

AN ANECDOTE

[417] It came about in the days of my stay in Malli that the sultan was angry with his senior wife, the daughter of his paternal uncle, who was called Qāsā which signifies the queen among them. The queen is his partner in the kingship, following the custom of the blacks. Her name is mentioned with his in the pulpit.[59]

The sultan imprisoned the queen in the house of one of the *farāriyya* [commanders] and appointed in her place his other wife, Banjū. She was not from among the daughters of the kings. The people discussed this a lot and disapproved of the action. The daughters of his paternal uncle visited Banjū to congratulate her on her queenship. They placed ashes on their arms but did not dust their heads. Then the sultan released

Qāsā from her bonds. The daughters of his paternal uncle visited her to congratulate her on her release and they dusted as is customary. Banjū complained to the sultan about this. [418] He became angry with the daughters of his paternal uncle and they were afraid of him and took refuge in the congregational Mosque. He forgave them and called them back. It is their custom when they go in to the sultan to strip themselves of their clothes and enter naked. They did this and he pardoned them. They then took to coming to the door of the sultan morning and evening for a period of seven days—as anyone does who is pardoned by the sultan. And Qāsā took to riding every day at the head of her slave girls and slaves with dust on their heads. She stopped by the place of audience covering her head, and nothing being seen but her face. The *amīrs* [officers] spoke much about her affair. The sultan gathered them to the place of audience and Dūghā said on his behalf, 'You have spoken a great deal concerning the matter of Qāsā, but she has committed a great crime.' Then he brought a slave woman of hers, fettered and shackled. She was ordered to tell what she knew. She reported that [419] Qāsā had sent her to Jaṭal, the son of the paternal uncle of the sultan, who had escaped him and gone to Kanburnī, to call him to dethrone the sultan from his kingdom.[60] And she said to him, 'I and all the askaris are under your orders.' When the *amīrs* [officers] heard this they said, 'This is a great crime and she deserves death for it.' Qāsā was afraid because of this and took refuge in the house of the preacher. It was their custom to take refuge in the mosque and if that were not possible, in the house of the preacher.

The blacks used to hate Mansā Sulaimān because of his

miserliness. Before him there was Mansā Maghā, and before Mansā Maghā, Mansā Mūsā. He was generous and noble and loved the white men and was kind to them. He is the one who gave Abū Isḥāq al-Sāḥilī in one day four thousand *mithqāls*. I was informed by a reliable person that he gave Mudrik ibn Faqqūṣ three thousand [420] *mithqāls* in one day—his grandfather Sāraq Jāṭa had been made a Muslim by the hand of the grandfather of this Mudrik.[61]

AN ANECDOTE

I was informed by this Mudrik the *faqīh* that a man from the people of Tilimsān [Tlemcen] known as ibn Shaikh al-Laban had been kind to the sultan Mansā Mūsā in his childhood, by giving him seven and one third *mithqāls*. He was then a young boy, not taken much notice of. Then it happened he came to him while he was sultan about a case. He recognized him and invited him forward and brought him near to himself so that he sat with him on the *banbī*. He then recalled what he had done for him. He said to his *amīrs* [officers], 'What is the reward for him who has done the good which he has done?' They said to him, 'For a good deed, ten like it. Give him seventy *mithqāls*.'[62] The sultan thereupon gave him seven hundred *mithqāls*, a robe of honour, slaves and servants [421] and ordered him to visit him often. I was told this story also by the son of ibn Shaikh al-Laban whom I have mentioned; this son was a scholar teaching the Qur'ān at Malli.

AN ACCOUNT OF WHAT I FOUND GOOD AMONGST THE BLACKS AND OF WHAT I DISLIKED

Amongst their good qualities is the small amount of injustice amongst them, for of all people they are the furthest from it. Their sultan does not forgive anyone in any matter to do with injustice. Among these qualities there is also the prevalence of peace in their country, the traveller is not afraid in it nor is he who lives there in fear of the thief or of the robber by violence. They do not interfere with the property of the white man who dies in their country even though it may consist of great wealth, but rather they entrust it to the hand of someone dependable among the white men until it is taken by the rightful claimant.

Another of the good habits amongst them is [422] the way they meticulously observe the times of the prayers and attendance at them, so also it is with regard to their congregational services and their beating of their children to instill these things in them.[63]

When it is Friday, if a man does not come early to the mosque he will not find a place to pray because of the numbers of the crowd. It is their custom for every man to send his boy with his prayer mat. He spreads it for him in a place commensurate with his position and keeps the place until he comes to the mosque. Their prayer-mats are made of the leaves of a tree like a date palm but it bears no fruit.

Among their good qualities is their putting on of good white clothes on Friday. If a man among them has nothing except a tattered shirt, he washes and cleans it and attends the Friday prayer in it. Another of their good qualities is their concern for learning the sublime Qur'ān by heart. They make fetters for their children when they appear on their part to be falling short in their learning of it by heart, and they are not taken off from them till they do learn by heart. I went in to visit the *qāḍī* on an ʿId day and his children [423] were tied up. I said to him, 'Why do you not release them?' He said, 'I shall not do so until they learn the Qur'ān by heart.' One day I passed by a handsome youth from them dressed in fine clothes and on his feet was a heavy chain. I said to the man who was with me, 'What has this youth done—has he killed someone?' The youth heard my remark and laughed. It was told me, 'He has been chained so that he will learn the Qur'ān by heart.'

Among the bad things which they do—their serving women, slave women and little daughters appear before people naked, exposing their private parts. I used to see many of them in this state in Ramaḍān, for it was the custom of the *farāriyya* [commanders] to break the fast in the sultan's house. Everyone of them has his food carried in to him by twenty or more of his slave girls and they are naked, every one. Also among their bad customs is the way women will go [424] into the presence of the sultan naked, without any covering; and the nakedness of the sultan's daughters—on the night of the twenty-seventh of Ramaḍān, I saw about a hundred slave girls coming out of his palace with food, with them were two of his daughters, they had full breasts and no clothes on. Another of their bad customs is their putting of dust and ashes on their heads as a sign of respect. And another is the laughing matter I mentioned of their poetic recitals. And another is that many of them eat animals not ritually slaughtered, and dogs and donkeys.

AN ACCOUNT OF MY JOURNEY AWAY FROM MALLI

My entry into Malli was on the fourteenth of the first month of Jumādā in the year '53 [i.e., 753 A.H., 28th June A.D. 1352], and my going out from there was on the twenty-second of Muḥarram in the year '54 [i.e., 754 A.H., 27 February A.D. 1353]. I was accompanied by a merchant known as Abū [425] Bakr ibn Yaʿqūb. We set out on the Mīma road. I was riding a camel because horses were dear, costing about one hundred *mithqāls* apiece. We reached a large arm of the river which comes out of the Nile and which cannot be crossed except in boats. That place has many mosquitoes and nobody passes through except at night.[64] We arrived at the arm of the river in the first third of the night and it was moonlight.

NOTE ON THE HORSES WHICH ARE IN THE NILE

When we arrived at the arm of the river, I saw on its bank sixteen beasts with enormous bodies. I was astonished by them. I thought they were elephants because there are plenty there. Then I saw them entering the river and said to Abū Bakr ibn Yaʿqūb, 'What beasts are these?' He said, 'These are horses of the river [hippopotami], they have come out [426] to graze on the dry land.' They are more thickset than horses and they have manes and tails, their heads are like the heads of horses and their legs like the legs of elephants. I saw these horses another time when we were travelling on the Nile from Tunbuktū to Kawkaw; they were swimming in the water and raising their heads and blowing. The boatmen feared them and came in close to the shore so as not to be drowned by them. They have a nice trick in hunting them, that is, they have spears with holes in them and put strong cords through these holes. They hit the horse with them; if by any chance the throw gets the foot or the neck, it goes through it and they pull him by the rope until they bring him to the bank. They kill him and eat his meat. There are great heaps of their bones on the river bank.

When we dismounted we stayed by this arm of the river in a large village ruled by a black governor who was a *hajji* and a gentleman and was called Farbā Magha̱. [427] He was one of those who had made the pilgrimage with sultan Mansā Musā when he made his pilgrimage.[65]

AN ANECDOTE

I was told by Farbā Māgha̱ā that when Mansā Musā arrived at this branch of the river there was with him a *qāḍī*, a white man, whose *kunya* was Abū 'l-ᶜAbbās, he was also known as al-Dukkālī [man of the Dukkāla tribe in Morocco]. The sultan gave him as a present four thousand *mithqāls* for his expenses. When they arrived at Mīma he complained to the sultan that the four thousand *mithqāls* had been stolen from him from his house. The sultan caused the *amīr* of Mīma to appear and threatened him with death if he did not present the man who stole the money. The *amīr* sought the thief and did not find anyone, for there are no thieves in their country. He entered the house of the *qāḍī* and was violent with his servants and threatened them. One of his slave girls said to him, 'He lost nothing, he only buried it [428] with his own hand in that place.' She pointed to the place. The *amīr* removed the gold and brought it to the sultan and told him the story. He was angry with the *qāḍī* and exiled him to the country of the unbelievers who eat human beings. He stayed among them four years. Then the sultan sent him back to his own country. The reason that he was not eaten by the unbelievers was his whiteness for they say that eating a white man is harmful because he is not ripe. The black man however is ripe according to them.[66]

AN ANECDOTE

There came to sultan Mansā Sulaimān a group of these blacks who eat human beings accompanied by one of their *amīrs*. According to their custom they had put in their ears large rings each of which was a span and a half across. They cover themselves in silk mantles. In their country there is a gold [429] mine. The sultan was gracious to them. He gave them as a hospitality gift a slave woman. They slaughtered her and ate her. They smeared their faces and hands with her blood and came to the sultan to return thanks. I was told that it is their custom to do that whenever they come to visit him. It was mentioned to me concerning them that they say that the tastiest meat in the flesh of women is the palm and the breast.

Then we departed from this village which is by the branch of the river I mentioned, and we arrived at the town of Qurī Mansa [or: the built up area of the villages of Mansa]. There my camel which I was riding died. When I was told by its keeper I came out to look at it. I found the blacks had eaten it as their custom is in eating a dead animal. I sent the two boys I had hired to serve me to buy me a camel at Zāgh̲arī which was a distance of about two days' journey. Some of the friends of Abū Bakr son of Yaʿqūb stayed with me while the latter went ahead to receive us [430] at Mīma. I stayed there [Qurī Mansa] for six days and was entertained by one of the pilgrims in this town until the two boys arrived with the camel.

AN ANECDOTE

In the days of my stay in this town I had a dream one night in which a person was saying to me, 'O Muḥammad, son of Baṭṭūṭa, why do you not read *sūra yāsīn* every day?' From that day I did not cease to read it every day whether I was travelling or remaining stationary.[67] Then I departed for the town of Mīma; in its neighbourhood we dismounted by some wells. We travelled then from there to the city of Tunbuktū, which is four miles from the Nile. Most of its inhabitants are Massūfa, people of the veil. Its governor is called Farbā Mūsā. I was present with him one day when he appointed [431] one of the Massūfa as *amīr* over a company. He placed on him a garment, a turban and trousers, all of them of dyed material. He then seated him on a shield and he was lifted up by the elders of his tribe on their heads. In this town is the grave of the unsurpassable poet Abū ʿIsḥāq al-Saḥilī of Gharnāta [Grenada], who is known in his own country as al-Ṭuwaījin.[68] There also is the grave of Sirāj al-Dīn ibn al-Ṭūwaik, one of the great merchants from among the people of Alexandria.

AN ANECDOTE

When sultan Mansa Mūsā made the pilgrimage, he stayed in a garden belonging to this Sirāj al-Dīn at Birkat al-Ḥabash [the Ethiopian's Pool] outside Cairo. The sultan lodged there and ran short of money. He borrowed it from Sirāj al-Dīn, and his *amīrs* also borrowed from him. Sirāj al-Dīn sent his representative with them to receive the money, but he stayed in Malli. [432] Then Sirāj al-Dīn himself went to get his money, accompanied by his son. When he reached Tunbuktū he was entertained by Abū ʿIsḥāq al-Saḥilī. It was fate that his death should come that night, and people talked about it, for they suspected that he was poisoned. His son said to them, 'I have eaten that food with him—that very same food. If there were poison in it we would all of us have been killed. But his allotted term had been completed.' His son arrived at Malli, received his money, and went back to Egypt.

At Tunbuktū I embarked on the Nile in a small vessel carved from one piece of wood. We used to come ashore every night in a village to buy what we needed of food and ghee in exchange for salt and perfumes and glass ornaments. Then I reached a town whose name I have been caused [by Satan] to forget. This town had as its *amīr* an excellent man, a pilgrim called Farbā Sulaimān, well known for his bravery and tenacity, no one was able [433] to bend his bow. I did not see among the blacks anyone taller than he nor more massive in body. In this town I needed some millet. I came to him on the birthday of the Apostle of God (may Allah grant him mercy and peace!).[69] I greeted him and he asked me about my arrival. There was with him a *faqīh* who was his scribe. I took a writing board which was before him and wrote on it, 'O *faqīh*, tell this *amīr* that we need some millet for our provisions. Greetings!' I handed over the board to the *faqīh* to read what was written on it privately and to speak to the *amīr* about it in his language. But he read it aloud and the *amīr* understood it. He took me by the hand and made me enter his audience room. In its were many weapons: shields, bows and spears. I found in his house a copy of the *kitāb al-mudhish* [the Book of the Astonishing] of ibn al-Jawzī, [434] and I began to read it.[70] Then a drink of theirs called *daqnū* was served. It is water with pounded millet mixed with a little honey or milk in it. They drink it instead of water, because if they drink the water by itself, it harms them.[71] If they have no millet, they mix it with honey or milk. Then a green melon was served and we ate from it.

A growing boy came in; the governor called him and said to me, 'Here is your hospitality gift. Guard him so that he does not run away.'[72] I took him and I wanted to turn away. He said, 'Stay till food is served.' An Arab slave girl of his from Damascus came in to us. She was an Arab and spoke to me in Arabic.

While we were in that place, we heard a loud crying in his house. He sent the slave girl to find out the news. She returned to him and informed him that a daughter of his had just died. He said, 'I do not [435] like mourning. Come, let us walk to the river,' meaning the Nile. He had houses on its banks. He brought out a mare and said to me, 'Ride!' But I said, 'I will not ride while you walk.' We walked together and reached his houses on the Nile. He brought out food and we ate. I bade him farewell and went away. I did not see among the blacks a person more generous or better than he. The boy he gave me is still with me up till now.

Then I travelled to the city of Kawkaw [Gao]. It is a big city on the Nile, one of the best of the cities of the blacks. It is one of the biggest and most fertile of their places, with much rice, milk, chicken and fish. In it there are *ʿinānī* pumpkins which have no rivals. The transactions of its people in buying and selling are carried out by means of cowries—as is the case among the people of Malli.[73] I stayed there about a month and was the guest of [436] Muḥammad ibn ʿUmar of the people of Miknāsa. He was a gentle person, fond of making jokes, a man of merit.[74] He died there after I left. I was also the guest there of *al-Ḥājj* Muḥammad al-Wajdī al-Tāzī who had travelled to Yaman, and of the *faqīh* Muḥammad al-Fīlālī, *imām* of the mosque of the whites.

Then I travelled from there in the direction of Takaddā [Takidda] in the hinterland [that is, away from the river] with a large caravan of the men of Ghadāmas [Ghadames in Libya] whose guide and leader was *al-Ḥājj* Wujjīn (the meaning of this word is 'jackal' in the language of the blacks).

I had a camel for riding and a she-camel for carrying provisions. When we set out on the first stage the she-camel broke down. *Al-Ḥājj* Wujjīn took what was on her and divided it among his companions. They shared out the burden. There was in the caravan a Maghribin [man of Arab north-west Africa] of the people of Tādalā who refused to carry any of it in the way other people had done. My servant lad was thirsty one day [437], I asked the Maghribin for water; he did not give it.

Then we arrived at the land of the Bardama people [a Tuareg

group], a tribe of the Berbers. The caravan cannot travel except under their protection; and amongst them the protection of a woman is more important than that of a man. They are nomads, they do not stay in one place. Their dwelling places are strange in form: they set up poles of wood and place mats around them, over that they put interwoven sticks and over them skins or cotton cloth. Their women are the most perfect of women in beauty and the most comely in figure, in addition to being pure white and fat. I did not see in the land anyone who attained to their standard of fatness. These women's food is cow's milk and pounded millet; they drink it mixed with water, uncooked, morning and evening. A man who wants to marry among them has to settle with them in the country near [438] them, and not take his spouse further than either Kawkaw or Īwālātan.

I was affected by sickness in this country because of extreme heat, being overcome by yellow bile. We exerted ourselves in travelling till we reached the city of Takaddā. There I lodged in the vicinity of the shaikh of the Maghribins, Saᶜīd ibn ᶜAlī al-Jazūlī. I was entertained by its *qāḍī*, Abū Ibrāhīm ᶜIsḥāq al-Jānātī, an eminent person. I was also the guest of Jaᶜfar ibn Muḥammad al-Massūfī. The houses of Takaddā are built of red stone. Its water supply flows over the copper mines and its colour and taste are changed by that fact. There is no cultivation there except a little wheat which is eaten by the merchants and visitors. It is sold at the rate of twenty of their *mudds* for a *mithqāl* of gold.[75] Their *mudd* is a third of the *mudd* in our country. Millet amongst them is sold at the rate of ninety *mudds* for a gold *mithqāl*. It is a country with many [439] scorpions. Its scorpions kill a child who has not reached puberty, whereas they rarely kill a man.[76] One day while I was there a scorpion stung a son of skaikh Saᶜīd ibn ᶜAlī in the morning. He died immediately and I attended his funeral [lit.: the carrying of the bier].

The people of Takaddā carry on no business but trading. Every year they travel to Egypt and bring from there everything there is in the country by way of fine cloths and other things. For its people ease of life and ample condition are supreme; they vie with one another in the number of slaves and servants they have—as likewise do the people of Malli and Īwālātan. They do not sell educated women-slaves, except very rarely and at a great price.

AN ANECDOTE

When I reached Takaddā I wanted to buy an educated woman-slave. I could not find one, then the *qāḍī*, Abū Ibrāhīm, sent me a slave-woman belonging to one of his friends.[77] [440] I bought her for twenty-five *mithqāls*. Then her master regretted the transaction and desired to cancel the sale. I said to him, 'If you direct me to another, I shall cancel the sale.' He directed me to a slave-woman of ᶜAlī ᶜAghyūl, who was the Maghribin from Tādallā who refused to transport any part of my luggage when my she-camel failed me, and refused to give a drink of water to my servant lad when he was thirsty. I bought her from him—she was better than the first woman I had bought and I cancelled the sale for my first friend. Then the Maghribin regretted having sold the slave-woman and desired a cancellation of the sale. He persisted in it; I refused so as to pay him back for his evil deed. He almost went mad or was about to perish out of grief. In the end, I cancelled the sale for him.

A NOTE ON THE COPPER MINE

There is a copper mine outside Takaddā. The people dig [441] for it in the earth, bring it to the town, and smelt it in their houses. This is done by their men, and the women-slaves. When they have smelted it into red copper, they make it into rods about the length of a span and a half: some are of fine gauge and some thick. The thick are sold at the rate of four hundred rods for a *mithqāl* of gold, the fine for six or seven hundred to the *mithqāl*: it is their means of exchange. They buy meat and firewood with the fine rods: they buy male and female slaves, millet, ghee, and wheat with the thick. Copper is carried from there to the city of Kūbar [Gobīr] in the land of the unbelievers, to Zaghay and to the country of Barnū (Bornu) which is at a distance of forty days from Takaddā. Its people are Muslim; they have a king whose name is Idrīs, who does not appear before the people nor speak to them except from behind a curtain.[78] From this country are brought [442] beautiful slave women and eunuchs and heavy fabrics. Copper is also taken from Takaddā to Jūjūwat and to the land of the Mūrtibīn and to other places.

ANECDOTE CONCERNING THE SULTAN OF TAKADDĀ

In the days of my stay in that place, the *qāḍī* Abū Ibrāhīm and the preacher Muḥammad and the teacher Abū Ḥafs and the shaikh Saʿīd ibn ʿAlī set out to call upon the sultan of Takaddā who was a Berber named Izār, and was at a distance of a day's journey from the town. A dispute had occurred between him and the Takarkurī who is also a sultan of the Berbers. The gentlemen I mentioned had gone to arbitrate between the two of them. I wanted to meet the sultan, so I hired a guide and set out towards him. He was informed by those gentlemen about my arrival and he came to me riding a mare without a saddle [443] as was their custom. In place of a saddle he had a fine red carpet. He had on a mantle, trousers, and a turban which were all blue. With him were the sons of his sister (they are those who will inherit his kingdom). We stood up for him and shook hands with him. He asked after my health and about my arrival, and was informed about these things. He lodged me in one of the houses of the Yanāṭibūn (they are like the domestic servants at home). He sent me a goat roasted on a spit and a wooden bowl of fresh cow's milk. Nearby to us was the tent of his mother and his sister and the two of them came and greeted us. His mother sent us fresh milk after dusk, which is their milking time. They drink it at that time and in the morning; but as to [normal] food, they do not eat it nor know of it. I stayed there six days and every day he sent two roast sheep—one in the morning and one in the evening. He was gracious to me in giving me [444] a she-camel and ten *mithqāls* of gold. Then I left him and returned to Takaddā.

RUINS OF THE OLD CITY FROM WHICH IBN BATTUTA SET OUT ON HIS CAMEL CARAVAN JOURNEY TO MALI. THESE WALLS WERE BUILT SOME CENTURIES AFTER HIS TRAVELS, BUT THIS WAS THE SITE OF THE 14TH CENTURY CITY
(Photo by Ross E. Dunn)

THE VALLEY OF THE WAD (RIVER) ZIZ NORTH OF THE RUINS OF SIJILMASA
(Photo by Ross E. Dunn)

THE MENTION OF THE ARRIVAL OF THE NOBLE COMMAND I RECEIVED

When I returned to Takaddā, the young slave of *al-Ḥājj* Muḥammad ibn Saᶜīd of Sijilmāsa arrived with a command from our master the commander of the faithful, the supporter of the faith, the depender on the Lord of the worlds, commanding me to appear in his sublime presence. I kissed the order and complied with it immediately. I bought two camels for my riding for thirty-seven and a third *mithqāls*. I wanted to travel to Tuwāt. I carried provisions for seventy nights since [normal] food is not to be found between Takaddā and Tuwāt, only meat and milk and ghee which are bought in exchange for cloth. I left Takaddā on Thursday, the eleventh of Shaᶜbān in the year [445] 'fifty-four [A.H. 754; 11th September A.D. 1353] in a big caravan which included Jaᶜfar al-Tuwātī, who is an eminent person, and the *faqīh* Muḥammad ibn ᶜAbd Allāh, *qāḍī* of Takaddā. In the caravan there were about six hundred slave-women.[79] We arrived at Kāhir in the land of the sultan of Karkarī. It is a land of plentiful grass. The people buy sheep there from the Berbers and cut the meat into strips. This is carried by the people of Tuwāt to their country.

From that land we entered into a wilderness with no buildings in it and no water: it is three days' journey. Then we travelled after that fifteen days through a wilderness which has no buildings but there is water. We reached the place from which the road to G͟hāt (which continues to Egypt) and the road to Tuwāt bifurcate. And there are there water-beds whose water flows over iron: when white cloths are washed in it, their colour becomes black. We travelled from there for ten [446] days, and arrived at the country of the Hakkar [Ahoggar] who are a tribe of the Berbers and wear face-veils. There is no good in them. We were met by one of their big men and he held up the caravan until they gave him cloths and other things. Our arrival in their country was in the month of Ramaḍān; they do not attack nor intercept caravans in it. When their robbers find property in the roads in Ramaḍān they do not bother about it, and it is likewise for all the Berbers who are along this road. We journeyed a month in the land of Hakkar: it has a scarcity of plants and an abundance of stones, the road too is rough.

On the day of ʿId al-Fitr [the festival of fast-breaking] we reached the land of some Berbers who are people of the veil like these [i.e., the Hakkar]. They gave us news of our country and told us that the Awlād K̲h̲arāj and the banī Yaghmūr had risen up, and set themselves up in Tasābīt in Tuwāt. [447] The people of the caravan were afraid because of this. Then we reached Būdā which is one of the biggest villages of Tuwāt. Its soil consists of sand and saline swamp. Its dates are plentiful but not sweet; yet its people prefer them to the dates of Sijilmāsa. There is no cultivation there, no ghee, no olive oil. These things are brought to it from the land of the Mag̲h̲rib. The food of its people is dates and locusts which are plentiful in their area. They preserve them as they store dates and feed on them. They go out to hunt locusts before sunrise when they cannot fly because of the cold.

We stayed at Būdā some days, then we travelled in a caravan and in the middle of D̲h̲ū' al-Qaʿda we arrived at the city of Sijilmāsa. I went out from it on the second of D̲h̲ū' al-Ḥijja [29 December A.D. 1353] during a period of fierce cold [448].

A lot of snow came down on the road. I have seen many rough roads and much snow in Būkhārā and Samarkand and in Khurāsān [in Persia] and in the land of the Turks, but I have never seen anything more difficult than the road of Umm Junaiba. We reached Dār al-Tamaᶜ on the night before ᶜId al-ᶜAḍḥā. I stayed there the day of the festival, then I left and arrived at the capital Fās, the residence of our master, the commander of the faithful, may God support him! I kissed his noble hand and received the good fortune of seeing his blessed face. I stayed in the protection of his goodness after long travels, may God The Exalted recompense him for what he has given me of great kindness and overwhelming benefit! May He make his day everlasting, and give the Muslims the pleasure of his long life!

Here ends the travel narrative called 'A Gift to the Onlookers concerning the Curiosities of the Cities and the Wonders of the Journeys.' The completion of its dictation was on the third Dhū al-Ḥijja of the year [449] '56 [756 A.H., 9 December A.D. 1355). Praise be to God and peace be on his servants whom he has chosen!

Ibn Juzayy says, 'Here ends the abridgement from the dictation of the shaikh Abū ᶜAbd Allāh Muḥammad ibn Baṭṭūṭa (may God be gracious to him!). . . .'[80]

NOTES TO TRANSLATION

1. The followers of Imām al Shāfiʿī constitute one of the four great rites or schools of law of the Sunni system. This remains the major school among Muslims in East Africa today. Its ways are characterized by a principled and traditionalist sunny common sense.

2. Zeila and Mogadishu are in modern Somalia. Ibn Baṭṭūṭa and his editor have an admirable way of giving a careful 'fix' of some of the place names and difficult words he uses by spelling out the vowels. We have omitted this spelling and used the spelling he gives, except in the case of Mombasa, where we give it in full to show what such vocalization is like. Where clear modern equivalents to place names exist we have given them in brackets. *Rāfiḍi* were those who rejected the first three Caliphs. They were probably Shiʿa of some kind. They may have been Zaidī. Seyyid Aktar Rizvi of Dar-es-Salaam thinks they may have been Ithnaʿasharī. Ibn Baṭṭūṭa was a staunch Sunni of the *Māliki* ma<u>dh</u>hab or school of law. He had little sympathy for non-Sunnis.

3. Richard Burton's *First Footsteps in East Africa,* edited by G. Waterfield and reissued, London, 1966, and the works of other Victorian travellers yield many interesting parallels and sidelights to ibn Baṭṭūṭa's narrative.

4. *Faqīh* and *qāḍī* are difficult to translate. The first relates to the study of Muslim law. The title Ll.D. in its medieval sense of a doctor of canon and other law in some ways describes a *faqīh,* though it might rank him too high in the academic scale for often it became simply a title of honor for a respected scholar. The *qāḍī* is the official judge to do with Muslim law appointed by the ruler. On both see J. Schacht: *An Introduction to Islamic Law,* Oxford, 1964.

5. *Sharīf:* a person who claims to be a descendant of the Prophet through Fāṭimā and ʿAlī. As such he can be given a place of honour in society and a share in alms. On the *sharīfs* see the Qurʾān VIII: 42, var-

ious *sharīf* family names in the *Encyclopaedia of Islam* and R. B. Serjeant: *The Saiyids of Hadramawt,* London, 1957.

6. This translates the Arabic as it stands. It may be a copyist's reading of the familiar *al Miṣrī* 'the Egyptian' for *al Muqrī*, the name of a family of jurists who were at the time established at this town. Ivan Hrbek, 'The Chronology of ibn Baṭṭuṭa's Travels', *Archiv Orientální* XXX, 1962, p. 412, based on Cerulli's article *Maḳdishū* in *Encyclopaedia of Islam.*

7. *Mawlānā* is still used by Muslims in East Africa as an address of respect for people of royal status or for religious leaders.

8. Betel leaves with areca nuts are still used in East Africa. *Panwallahs* offer various 'chews' costing from a few cents to a dollar. Presumably then, as now, direct Indian influence had its effect.

9. At an East African *mawlidi* or celebration in honour of the birth of the Prophet, a *mrashi* is still used to sprinkle the people with perfumed water.

10. *Wazir* is another title with a range of meanings covering the spectrum from a Prime Minister to an officer in charge of some function in the royal kitchen. In ibn Baṭṭūṭa 'official' is as good a translation as any. He seems to confine the title *amīr* to military officers of unspecified rank.

11. 'Ghee' is a Hindustani word which has come into English. It is a cooking fat made from milk. 'Large wooden dish': Arabic *ṣahfah.* Compare Kiswahili *chano,* a shallow wooden dish on which various foods can be set forth. The word translated 'fish' a little lower down is the same word used in the Qur'ān to describe the great fish which swallowed Jonah. H. F. Janssens in his *Ibn Batouta,* Brussels, 1948, commends Gibb's remark that our author was a 'geographer despite himself.' His own remark that this work is 'un atlas gastronomique de l'Orient' (p. 89) as well as his lively account of the life and times of the author deserves commendation. He regrets that the great traveller's religion precluded his enjoyment of the local wines.

12. Much of this description of food would apply to hospitality on the East Coast to this day. Ibn Baṭṭūṭa may have mistaken the coconut milk used in cooking the banana for fresh milk. Regarding mangoes, the usual Arabic word today is *manaj*—to which 'mango' would appear to be related, though it is said the word came into European languages from South Indian. His word *ʿanbah* and its collective *ʿanbūn* (compare *tamar, tamrūn*: dates) are related to Kiswahili *-embe* and both may have some connection with the antecedent of the Hindi *anb,* Urdu *āmb.* The word translated 'chillies' is *fulfil,* compare Kiswahili *pilipili.*

13. 'The royal enclosure': after Muʿāwiyya escaped the attack in the mosque to which ʿAlī succumbed, Muslim monarchs sometimes provided themselves with an enclosure to protect them at prayer.

14. It would be natural if some corruption crept into the text of descriptions of exotic clothes and foods. Dr. Humphrey Fisher has here, and in other places, corrected our text and we have adopted his suggestions. His note here reads as follows: 'Gibb says "with fine robes of Egyptian stuffs with their appendages (?) underneath it," and suggests a copyist's error distorting an original *mutarrazāt,* "embroideries." The Beirut (1960) edition says *tarūhāt* which are something thrown over the shoulders, whence my suggested word "loose".' The panoply of kingship is most interesting. One is reminded of an Ashanti *durbar* when the kings walked with dignity beneath state umbrellas. In Ghana the four canopies were superimposed on the same carrying handle and one bird presided over all. It is possible that the umbrella came to African kings from the Hindu god-kings. Some commentary on African sacral ruler-cult is also given in the section on the visit to Malli.

15. The difference between the cases decided by the *qāḍī* and those decided by the group may have been the difference between the law of the *sharīʿa* which was known to the *qāḍī* as an expert who had to set out what the law said, and traditional law where a group of old men who knew many cases and precedents would give a verdict on behalf of customary law.

16. *Bilād as-sawāhil:* our author's use would indicate that he thought of it as a land south from Mombasa, including the coasts of what we would now call northern Tanzania and perhaps the islands. Having sailed past Lamu, Malindi and Gedi out at sea, ibn Baṭṭūṭa first touched the lands we would associate with the word 'Swahili' at Mombasa. Kilwa would be towards their southern side, but the Islands of the Moon (Comoro) were perhaps excluded. On the use of the expression 'the coast lands' we may compare the use of *mrima* in Mombasa: people going over the causeway refer to the mainland as *mrima.* The student will find G. S. P. Freeman-Grenville's *The East African Coast, Select Documents,* Oxford, 1962, and *The Medieval History of the Coast of Tanganyika,* London, 1962, well worth consulting. The root *z-n-j* remains a mystery. As used here, it seems to indicate the black people of the East African coast and islands. J. O. Hunwick's 'The term *zanj* and its derivatives in a West African chronicle' in D. Dalby, ed., *Language and History in Africa,* 1970, pp. 102–108, is not relevant to the East African meaning. *Zunūj,* the form used here, is of course a plural and refers to the people. On 'the land of Zinj or Zanj" compare *bilād as-sudān.* We had considered using *Zinj* or *Zanj* but finally decided to keep the plural. *Kulwa*-'Kilwa' is more usual. His Manbasaʿ is more correct than 'Mombasa.'

17. Mombasa is an island close to the mainland. Ibn Baṭṭūṭa says it has no *barr*—hinterland, meaning no mainland dependencies. Today going up to the hinterland (in Kiswahili *bara)* in Mombasa can include almost anywhere in Kenya and Uganda. The great traveller was there only a short time. It is indeed unlikely that there was no cultivation there, probably he means the cultivation of normal cereals. The banana had, as he states, already reached the Sawaḥil (from Indonesia perhaps via Madagascar). It is probable that he is mistaken over the mosques being made of wood. It seems likely that the mosques were of stone. Perhaps he used some rare word for coral which scribes changed to a more familiar word, or the mosques had wooden facings. Most probably his memory deceived him. His description of certain ways of carrying out the ablutions at Mombasa is most accurate. The *kata,* a ladle made out of half a coconut or an

empty jam can with a handle stuck through it, is still used. Modern religious scholars coming from Mombasa say there is more footwear there today, but add modestly that the high standards of integrity and religion have inevitably wilted a little before an influx of foreigners.

18. *Jammūn: Hobson-Jobson,* that magnificent dictionary of the Anglo-Indian language edited by Yule and Burnell, has recently been reissued and enables us to recognize this as *eugenia jambolana.* Various things sweet and plum-like seem to be able to carry the name. Cf. also Platt's *Dictionary of Urdu and Classical Hindi s.v. janbu,* the rose-apple.

19. Kilwa has been extensively excavated. Neville Chittick's report in *Azaania* I, 1966, pp. 1–36, gives an account of the work and a full bibliography. Even in ruins it is an impressive site on its island. When ibn Baṭṭūṭa visited it it must indeed have been one of the fairest towns in tropical Africa or indeed the world. It would seem it depended for its prosperity on the slave and ivory trade converging on it from the Rufiji and Ruvuma routes in the direction of Lake Malawi as well as on its position as a staging post in the gold trade through Sofala with *regnum Monomotapiae* and the gold producing areas in the Sofala hinterland. The Portuguese sacked the city in 1507 and broke the links in the north-south gold trade. Various wild tribes broke down the inland trade. Kilwa has never recovered, not even in its late Arab form of Kilwa Kivinje or the colonial Kilwa Masoko. H. A. R. Gibb, *The Travels of Ibn Baṭṭūṭa,* Hakluyt Series, vol. II, Cambridge, 1962 (abbreviated hereafter as Hakluyt II), p. 380, note 61, takes it Yūfī is Nupe and that ibn Baṭṭūṭa has confused the gold dust of the Niger with the mined gold of Sofala. It is possible that ibn Baṭṭūṭa or, more likely, his editor, did confuse things in this way. Possibly we shall discover that there was inland from Sofala a source of gold with a name like Yūfī. We shall meet Yūfī again in the West African section.

20. Defrémery and Sanguinetti's *Variantes et Notes* at page 455 give a number of variants for j-*n-d.* Gibb (Hakluyt II, p. 380, note 59) accepts j-*n-w* and connects it with the word which came into European languages as 'Guinea,' roughly the non-Muslim forest and coastal belt of West Africa. We prefer to leave it unidentified.

21. *Kunya*: this is the Arabic term for an additional name given to someone—'son of','father of'. It can be extended to physical features 'father of the forked beard' or to features of character, as in this case. Both the writers on meeting this one,'father of grants', thought of certain officials of the Rockefeller Foundation who had enabled us as scholars of religion to imitate ibn Baṭṭūṭa in a small way.

22. Gibb (Hakluyt II, p. 382, note 67) reckons ibn Baṭṭūṭa probably left Kilwa with the southwest monsoon about the end of March. According to old East African dhow travellers, he would take four weeks to reach Arabia or a little more for India.

23. For general background reading to this section of the *Travels* there is an extensive number of books. The relevant part of Gibb's Hakluyt series has now appeared, but see his selections in Broadway Travellers series published in 1929 and reprinted a number of times. We refer to it as *Selections.* We would recommend especially E. W. Bovill's *Caravans of the Old Sahara* which was re-written and re-issued in 1958 as *The Golden Trade of the Moors.* W. D. Cooley's *The Negroland of the Arabs,* London, 1841, reprinted 1966, does not help the non-expert much. C. Monteil, *Les empires du Mali,* Paris, 1929, reprinted 1968; D. T. Niane, *Recherches sur l'empire du Mali au moyen âge,* Conakry, 1962, and R. Mauny, V. Monteil, A. Djenidi, S. Robert, J. Devisse, *Extraits tires des voyages d'Ibn Baṭṭūṭa,* Dakar, 1966 (abbreviated as Mauny *et al. Extraits),* are most helpful. Nehemia Levtzion's writing is also most relevant—the article in the *Journal of African History* which we cite below;'The Early States of the Western Sudan to 1500' which appears as a chapter in J. F. A. Ajayi and M. Crowder's *History of West Africa,* London, 1971, as well as his important book *Ancient Ghana and Mali,* London, 1973, and a paper on 'The differential impact of Islam among the Soninke and Manding' given at a conference on Manding Studies held at the London School of Oriental and African Studies in the summer of 1972. A number of the other papers presented have bearing on the subject and have been made available in mimeographed form.

24. The Massūfa were one of the major tribes of Berber nomads who

inhabited the Sahara. *Anlī* is a name of Berber origin for a kind of small-grained millet that was probably independently domesticated in West Africa. The botanical name is *pennisetum typhoideum.* For botanical information see J. M. Dalziel, *The Useful Plants of West Tropical Africa,* London, 1937. His indices of vernacular terms, scientific and common names make his book most useful. A. P. Murdock, *Africa, Its Peoples and Their Culture History,* New York, 1959, has a lot of information on the history of plants but only carries an index of tribal names.

25. *Mithqāl:* a measure of weight, in this case, for weight in gold. It is difficult to determine an equivalence. M. G. C. Miles *(The Coinage of the Umayyads of Spain,* two volumes, New York, 1950) and Lévi-Provencal *(Histoire de l'espagne musulmane,* vol. III, Paris, 1953) give various opinions, but on the whole it looks as if in our author's time in the west the *mithqāl* weighed about 4.6 to 4.8 grammes. Mauny *et al., Extraits,* p. 36, value it at 39.295 French francs of 1964. The *qinṭar* mentioned just further on was in Egypt the equivalent of 44.93 kilogrammes and in Tunisia to 53.9. (Compare French *quintal* and Latin *centenarius).* See also Walter Hinz, *Islamische Masse und Gewichte,* Leiden, 1955.

26. Mauny *et al., Extraits,* p. 37, say this distance was about 250 kilometres.

27. Tāsarahlā is located by Mauny *et al., Extraits,* p. 38 and map on p. 32, as 250 km. due south of Taghāzā and 480 km. north northeast from Īwālātan. *Takshīf:* literally 'the discovery,' hence 'the uncoverer' or 'scout'.

28. The *Farba* as representing the king would partake in part of his sacral monarchy. He was sitting perhaps under some kind of arched lintel and like many West African monarchs spoke through a 'spokesman' or herald (cf. the Ghanaian *okyeame* who is used even when the king speaks to his own people). It was not insolence but normal local good manners. Ibn Baṭṭūṭa was, alas, not the last white man to regret his arrival; luckily Africans overlook such over-hasty

feelings based on ignorance, and most often the worst culprits among the strangers come to look back on their visit with appreciation.

29. Manshā Jū is probably *mansā dyon,* meaning 'servant of the king.' It is indeed surprising that a seasoned traveller such as our author did not grasp the symbolism of a fellowship meal where the staple food together with milk and honey were served. Apart from the offering of the basic and the pleasantest food, it signified that no black arts would be used against one and reciprocally it meant the recipient would behave loyally. Probably ibn Baṭṭūṭa's age and eminence were weighing him down and he expected special treatment.

30. Many sub-Saharan African tribes are matrilineal; as the Akan proverb says, 'Everybody knows who a person's mother is.' It is a matter of the blood being provided by the mother. To a child, the mother's brother is the most important male in the group. This has led to a great deal of friction where this kind of society has met Islam (and indeed, western society). Islam, on the whole, has been extremely tolerant and patient, but in the end the change-over has come. It is still possible to trace it in process amongst living informants, for instance among the Yao of south-west Tanzania. African society has been even more tenacious in refusing to bring its women-folk into a position of apparent bashful withdrawal, and African Muslims may be heard to say this is not essential to Islam as a religion, but is part of the cultural vessel.

31. On the journey between Walata and Malli see the paper read at the London Manding Conference of 1972 by Claude Meillassoux. This scholar, who appears to be familiar with the actual topography, presents a number of valuable alternatives as well as probable sites, a detailed bibliography, and a sketch map. See also his article in *The Journal of African History,* vol. XIII, 3, 1972, pp. 389–595.

32. This is a note by ibn Juzayy, ibn Baṭṭūṭa's editor, who came from Spain. Our traveller is obviously speaking of that magnificent feature of parts of the African landscape, the baobab. See Dalziel, *Useful Plants,* pp. 112f. Ibn Baṭṭūṭa's picture of travel through West Africa

remains strangely true to this day despite the coming of the 'mammy wagon', the motor lorry, which almost more than any other material thing has transformed West Africa. One can see the market women with their pounded foods, their calabashes and almost read the counterpart of the notice 'carved calabash is here'.

33. People at Mombasa take the baobab fruit and pound it into a kind of flour. This fruit looks rather like a cucumber or outsize sausage.

34. *Ghartī:* soninké: ***kharite,*** shea butter. The tree is to be seen dotted about in the West African savannah, somehow surviving the bush-fires and the goats. The women collect the nuts, prepare and sell the oil. A few thousand of them in a market is a sight never to be forgotten. With ibn Baṭṭūṭa's remarks we may compare Dalziel's (p. 353) 'if clarified, native-prepared shea butter can be used quite acceptably for European cooking'. To the uses ibn Baṭṭūṭa gives, add 'to pomade the hair and to make a soap'.

35. *Tāsirghant:* a word of Berber derivation; the root of ***telephium imperati*** which grows in the Maghrib, and is used in perfumery. Though some of the forms of maize, some beans, root-crops, groundnuts, etc., so prominent in West Africa today are descended from crops introduced from the Americas, West Africa carried out her own agricultural revolution in prehistoric times and there were indigenous counterparts and predecessors to most of the immigrant varieties. ***Kuskus (couscous)*** is still well known in North Africa. It is a wheat or groats made into a paste and cooked. Meat or vegetables are served with it. ***Nabaq*** is a Christ's thorn ***(ziziyphus spinachristi)*** whose fruit (called in English 'lotus') can be dried and made into a flour. ***Fonio*** is a cereal like semolina. The problem over the rice is a puzzle unless it was a native variety with some poison in its skin which had to be cooked a very long time, or perhaps the danger feared was beri-beri. A little further on ibn Baṭṭūṭa tells how he ate a kind of *qalqās*—colocasia, coco-yam, or similar edible root—which almost killed him. Probably it had not been cooked long enough.

36. The Kẖārijites were those early Muslims who separated themselves from those who submitted divine matters to human arbitra-

tion. The ruling class in the 'Umānī sultanate of Zanzibar were Ibādi. Ivor Wilkes says the Sag͟hanag͟hū are 'a specialized "clerical" lineage existing in symbiotic relationship with the Dyula groups, whose association, historically, has been with commerce. They are widely spread in West Africa, particularly in the Ivory Coast and western Upper Volta.' *(Research Bulletin of the Centre of Arabic Documentation* II, 2, Ibadan, 1966, pp. 11f.)

37. *Māliki* refers to the Sunni school of law which remains dominant in West Africa. Both ibn Baṭṭūṭa and his editor belonged to it. *Tūrī* is a patronymic still used in West Africa for a number of 'marabutic' lineages. In the beginning it may have referred to their sacral status or origin but today it is very loosely employed.

38. Zāg͟ha is probably Diagha at the south-west edge of the Masina flood-plain. The other places named, where no equivalent is given to them below in brackets, are not directly identifiable. Where a reasonable guess at their location is possible, they are named on the map.

39. Ibn Baṭṭūṭa takes it that the great river of West Africa is the Nile and that it continued eastward from where he last saw it in West Africa to the highest point where he had seen the Nile; that is, in Upper Egypt. It was a pardonable mistake based on what he had seen with his own eyes, what was reported to him, and the natural human and scientific desire to accept the most simple hypothesis to explain observed phenomena. His remarks on religion in Nubia are particularly interesting, for they indicate the survival of Christianity, though the monarch of Dongola, their great stronghold, had become Muslim. Recent excavations before the flooding caused by the Aswan Dam will no doubt add much to our knowledge. The periodical *Kush* has since 1963 carried most fascinating reports and serves as a guide to the mass of other literature appearing. *Al-malik al-nāṣir* is probably the *mamlūk* sultan of Egypt, Muḥammad, known as the victorious ruler, who ruled Egypt thrice, 1293–4, 1298–1308 and 1309–40.

40. The River Ṣanṣara: Mauny *et al. (Extraits,* p. 49f.) and M. Delafosse ('Le Gana et Mali et l'emplacement de leurs capitales', *Bulletin du*

comite d'etudes historiques et scientifique de l'A.O.F., 1924, pp. 528f.) take it that this is probably the River Sankarani which runs into the Niger 80 kilometres southwest of Bamako.They add that the word *Mali* is of *soninke* origin and signifies 'the capital'.A summary of the debate will be found in J. O. Hunwick's paper 'The Mid-Fourteenth Century Capital of Mali' read at the Manding Conference of 1972. He concludes that it is not possible yet to pinpoint the location accurately but 'attention should be concentrated on the left bank of the Niger, downstream from Bamako to about as far as Niamina'. See also his article in *The Journal of African History* XIV, 2, 1975, pp. 195-208.

41. On the various details mentioned by our author in connection with dynastic politics in Malli see Nawal Bell's paper presented to the Manding Conference on 'The Age of Mansā Mūsa of Mali: Problems in Succession and Chronology', and N. Levtzion: 'The thirteenth and fourteenth century kings of Mali', *Journal of African History* IV, 3, 1961, pp. 341-353. Levtzion shows by studying other sources, especially ibn K͟haldūn, that our author was somewhat confused about collateral branches of the royal family and the intrigues going on; for instance, the rivalry between the house of Mansā Mūsa and the house of his brother Mansā Sulaimān. The genealogical table given by Levtzion makes the matter clear. For our purposes here it is probably sufficient to mention the following points:

(1) The Sāriq-Djāṭa whom our author says was converted to Islam and was Mansā Mūsa's grandfather is to be identified with the first Mārī-Djāṭa who was a *brother* of Mūsa's grandfather. Mūsa's line was collateral to this Mārī-Djāṭa's line.

(2) After Mūsa's (1312-37) death his successor Mansā Mag͟hā ruled for only a few years before the power was taken over by Mūsa's brother Sulaimān. Sulaimān died in 1360 and before long his successor was deposed by Mūsa's line.

(3) Ibn Baṭṭūṭa says the Qāsā appealed to Djātal. Levtzion states that Sulaimān succeeded in thwarting this plot in 1352 or 1353, but seven years later his successor was deposed by another Mārī-Djāṭa (1360-73) who belonged to Mūsa's line and may be identified with our author's 'Djātal.'

Most people familiar with medieval history and the complications of merging matriarchal systems, let alone rotating succession, would give ibn Baṭṭūṭa high marks for his performance under such a test, especially when competing with an historical genius such as ibn K͟haldūn whose findings may yet be given pause when oral tradition has been properly collated.

42. The deceased was the Marinid sultan of Fez who reigned till 1351. Muslim honorifics to most westerners are quaint and redolent of the East of romance. East African Muslims like to know their proper use and often interject them most correctly into addresses and recitations as a kind of antiphonal response. Here is a concise guide to some of them:

(1) 'May God be pleased with him,' after the name of a person to be honoured religiously.

(2) 'The Exalted', 'the Most High', after the name of God.

(3) 'May God grant him blessing and peace,' (in printing abbreviated to S.A.W. on the basis of the Arabic initial letters) after the name of the Prophet Muḥammad.

(4) 'Upon him, peace,' after the name of prophets other than Muḥammad.

(5) 'May God have mercy on him,' after the name of someone dead. Where living and dead are prayed for together, the prayer is for forgiveness for the dead and for the living, long life. 'Reading stools': *al-rabaʿ-āt* may rather be boxes or biers used for a kind of memorial 'funeral'.

43. There are various ceremonies including alms-giving connected with the 27th, *lailat al-qadr,* the night of power when angels descend with blessing. The local use on which ibn Baṭṭūṭa is commenting is that there they call it *zakāt,* though normally that applies to the legal alms proper. Compare the northern Nigerian use *of ṣalla (salāt)* for a particular public festival prayer when its regular use is for the prescribed daily prayers.

44. *Zardk͟hana:* Said Hamdun remarked 'this word has a Persian air', if so, it may have to do with yellow embroidered robes. It may be a kind of silk embroidered with the forms of animals.

45. 'Pages': this word is used to indicate boys and young men at an African court. For instance at Kabaka Muteesa's court these lads from all over Buganda, not necessarily of royal or aristocratic blood, learnt the business of government and afterwards went out as chiefs and royal officials.

46. In various parts of Africa the king sits on a platform made of earth which is raised a few feet above the surrounds but is large enough to allow a certain number of people to stand on it around the main person. Probably the *banbī* was such a platform which could perhaps mean also 'seat of government'. The word is probably related to the Mandinke *bembe,* bench, platform.

47. *Shaṭr:* this is translated 'umbrella' though it is in Arabic an unusual word. Perhaps it is related to the Indian word which appears in Gujerati as *chtri,* the umbrella being an ancient emblem of kingship in India. Silken umbrellas topped by emblems such as birds are still carried over Akan kings in Ghana.

48. *Mutanfas:* it is difficult to say exactly what kind of cloth this was. By 'Roman' an Arab writer could mean 'Byzantine' or use it to mean very much what Africans today mean by the word 'European'. There was a good amount of trade between the lands subject to Constantinople, various parts of Italy and the islamic world in the fourteenth century.

49. *Qanābir:* probably represents *ganābir* (singular *ganbri)* which are like the two-stringed guitars still used in North Africa. Farmer's *History of Arabian Music,* London, 1929, reprinted in 1967, mentions instruments of this kind, such as the *qītāra* used in al-Andalus.

50. The account of kingship customs is strongly reminiscent of the Byzantine ceremonial connected with the king in his *consistorium,* the ceremony of *proskynēsis* and the victory cult. (See N. Q. King: *There's Such Divinity Doth Hedge a King,* London, 1960.) This is not necessarily to imply that African kingship copied the Byzantine, though the Nubian kingdoms could have received and transmitted such influences. Similar ceremonies could be witnessed in Uganda at

Mmengo, Hoima and Mbarara till 1966. As Professor S. H. Hooke admitted in his eighty-sixth year, 'spontaneous generation seems a simpler solution than diffusion'. In any case, one has to be on one's guard against saying pure African traditional kingship was autocratic. In certain cases as a result of disintegration or recent manoeuvres by the monarch it could become tyrannous. With regard to the 'dusting', this is found quite often in East African circumcision rituals as a means of warding off misfortune at a time of exposure or when the numinous is present in uncovered and raw form. Though abject ruler-cult obtruded itself in certain islamic kingdoms, Islam tends to deprecate such customs. It is said that it was a certain Muslim (Arab or Swahili) who was the first to dare to rebuke a Kabaka for executing his subjects, pointing out that he and they were subjects of Allah.

Ibn Baṭṭūṭa at another place (IV 302f.—while describing customs in China) mentions that some of the people of the land of the blacks, when their king dies, dig a deep tomb and bury with him some of the king's friends, slaves, the children of noblemen, and vessels full of food. They break the arms and the legs of the victims. One of the Massūfa who was living among the people of the land of Kūbar (Gobir) had difficulty in saving his son from being buried alive with the sultan who had recently died. Archaeology has shown this was a custom carried on without any possibility of cultural diffusion in many different parts of the world.

51. The description of the shape of festival ritual in Islamic Africa in the fourteenth century may prove to be of as great interest to comparative liturgiologists as Saint Luke's synagogue service at Nazareth or Saint Ambrose's basilican service when he was able to exhort and rebuke the emperor.

52. *Ṭailasān:* the word is still used at Mombasa to indicate the white headgear of the prayer leader or Friday preacher. In West Africa it can indicate the light cotton head and shoulder covering worn by the learned among the Muslims.

53. Arabic: *yūhallilūn wa yukabbirūn.*

54. In 1965 a manuscript notebook of the late Shaikh Sekyim-wanyi,

who is reputed to have been the first *muganda* to make the pilgrimage, was brought to Makerere. It contained sermon notes in Arabic for use at the great Festivals and the subjects covered were much the same as those mentioned by ibn Baṭṭūṭa. Probably they are just about the same everywhere in the Islamic world.

55. Just as there are festal days differentiated from the ferial and associated with the octaves of certain great Christian festivals, so there are special days associated with the great Islamic festivals. These are usually two days after the feast itself, which with the day itself make a triad.

56. Ingenious African historians in search of pre-colonial datings usesuch data as the spread of the banana and the xylophone. It is probable that an instrument as complicated as this would be introduced or invented in one place and then spread by diffusion. Circumcision of adolescents or deformation of ox horns could probably be discovered spontaneously in many places.

57. These are the famous Manding *griots* or bards, men of the reciter class. The custom of 'poets' and 'singers' standing before kings to recite the deeds of the past and the king's own deeds, is ancient and widespread in Africa. In a pre-literate society, till Muslim scribes began to write down these things, they were the 'memories' and historians of the community. Their task was no laughing matter for in many places if they stumbled in the recitation or made a mistake, they paid for it with their lives. They also had the fearful privilege of bringing aberrations from the past to the attention of the king and by their cult of victory ensuring victory. They often wore costumes, partly to put on a *persona* to show they did not speak as individuals in their own right, but more because spirits came and dwelt in them. It is doubtful whether the hobby horse in English May-day ceremonial was considered ridiculous in the days when morris dancing was not a mere revival.

The word translated 'a bird' is *al-shaqshāq,* which probably represents *al-shaqrāq,* a bird of speckled green, red and white found around Mecca (Al Fairūzabadi: *al-Qāmūs al Muhīṭ).* Which African bird is intended, one cannot be sure.

58. This account reminds one of certain forms of Semitic prophecy and divination (see Guillaume's book of that title, London, 1938). The pious man beholds the locusts, in number, they are *too great (Ar. kathīr),* this causes a voice to impinge upon his consciousness to say that they come to punish the *too great (yakthuru)* wrong in the land. Compare Amos who sees the *awake* tree and hears a voice saying God is *awake:* and locusts in the Hebrew Bible and the Qur'ān as punishers of wrong.

59. For a Muslim of ibn Baṭṭūṭa's type, this would be most unusual. *Kāsa* in Mandinke indicates the queen or first wife of the ruler. The 'woman-king' is often important in African kingship. She was a sovereign in her own right. Often she was not in fact the king's spouse but a female monarch chosen from the princesses of the blood royal. We may be in this narrative witnessing the sultan's attempt to replace the African type of queen by the consort-type of queen, a person who owed her position to her husband.

60. *Jaṭal* probably represents the Mandinka *dyata,* 'lion', a fairly common name, but see the note above on dynastic politics in Malli.

61. Mansā Mūsa brought Abū Isḥāq, who came from Grenada, back with him from Mecca. Ibn Baṭṭūṭa was shortly to visit the latter's grave at Timbuktu. At the London Manding Conference of 1972, J. O. Hunwick presented a paper about him entitled 'An Andalusian in Mali'.

62. Cf. Qur'ān VI: 161, 'The man that does good shall receive tenfold.'

63. A tradition tells us to encourage a child to pray at seven and beat him at ten if he does not.

64. Ibn Baṭṭūṭa was going northeastwards towards Timbuktu along the great bend of the river system. He seems to have met two of Africa's great enemies and guardians, the tsetse fly (which made horses dear) and the mosquito (which kept out white men). The latter bite more at night than in the day so some other insect may be intended. On the method of hippopotamus hunting which he mentions, see J. P. Rouch: *Les Songhay,* Paris, 1954, pp. 21–22. The method was apparently still

in use on parts of the Niger Bend till prohibited by the colonial authorities.

65. This famous pilgrimage took place in 1324 and 1325.

66. It is amazing how ingenuous and gullible this experienced traveller can be: he passes on these excellent stories to prove white men are both immature and dishonest, both told with obvious gusto and laughter by his sophisticated African informant. Later, when some people make a meal of his camel, they tell him it had died, he rushes out to find they have already eaten it. His only emotion is disgust at their eating a dead animal.

67. This is Chapter XXXVI of the Qur'ān and is still read daily by many Muslims especially in commemoration of a dead friend or relative or as a *memento mori* for themselves. It is perhaps a sign that our author realized that he was getting old and his death was drawing near. We may compare the use of Psalm XXIII or John XIV by some Christians.

68. Gibb's *Selections* renders this as 'Little Saucepan.'

69. 'The birthday of the Prophet': the *maulid* is very popular in East Africa today. If the celebration of the birthday was brought into *mamlūk* Egypt by analogy with Christmas, this mention of it illustrates how closely the land of the blacks was linked to Egypt in matters Islamic.

70. It is a comment on the distribution of books in the medieval Islamic world to find a theological work written in Baghdad about a century and a half earlier being read by a West African. The avidity with which ibn Baṭṭūṭa takes it up evokes the sympathy of any who have to travel when they want to study. Ibn al-Jawzī is described as a Ḥanbalite who died in 597/1200. The book was a compilation of Qur'ānic knowledge and tradition.

71. In West Africa one is still assured by a number of the Scots medical men who serve there that the water is dangerous. It seems that statistics prove more die there by drinking the water than by whisky.

72. 'Growing boy': the Arabic literally means 'five spans high', i.e., not fully grown.

73. 'Cowries': these shells used to be used as currency in various parts of Africa. Today they are used in ritual ornaments, the Comparative Religions person's usual imaginative explanation being that they are fertility symbols. The shells themselves are supposed to have come from the Indian Ocean, though how in antiquity they reached West Africa from there is a puzzle. Ibn Baṭṭūṭa mentions them while in the Maldives [IV 121]. He remarks that at Malli and Jūjū (Gao) they were sold at a thousand, one hundred and fifty for a gold dinar. See also Marion Johnson, 'The cowrie currencies of West Africa', *Journal of African History,* vol. XI, 1970, pp. 17-49, 331-353.

'inānī: whether this indicates a type of pumpkin or a place which grows them, it has not been possible to establish.

74. This is as graceful and pleasing a compliment as any host could hope to earn.

75. The *mudd* is a variable cubic measure. Taking the *shenbul* as our unit, the *mudd* was about one-sixth of it; that is, perhaps it was equivalent to eighteen litres. (*Shenbul* may be related to the word 'bushel' and *mudd* to the Latin *modius.*) The estimates of various scholars consulted vary from 0.75 litres to 46.6.

76. Early in a sojourn in West Africa a good steward will explain to the tenderfoot: 'Scorpion injection go killee pickin'; trouble man, pain pass all.'

77. As Evelyn King remarked: 'Nowadays one has to offer them marriage.'

78. A number of monarchs in north-eastern Nigeria have retained this custom of speaking from behind curtains down to modern times. It is one of the traits of divine kingship picked out for instance in Tor Istram: *The King of Ganda*, Stockholm, 1944. In connection with the recruitment of slaves, one of the writers was amazed to discover at Salaga in North Ghana old men who had witnessed the creation of eunuchs for service in the Turkish imperial service.

79. This is the full title according to the flowery custom of the day; but the work is more familiarly known as the *Ribla,* which may be rendered, 'the travel-narrative', or 'travels'. Ibn Juzayy's remark on ibn Baṭṭūṭa, 'May God be gracious to him', indicates that the latter was still alive when he wrote his conclusion to the work.

APPENDIX I
WEST AFRICA

Dedicated in memoriam
Professor Nehemia Levtzion, 1935-2003

One evening, perhaps a quarter of a century ago, it was my privilege to sit down to dinner with Nehemia Levtzion in the gardens of Akuafo Hall in the University of Ghana, Legon. The "Akuafo" gives thanks to the munificence of the Ghanaian cocoa farmer. The fragrance of the jasmine, the redness of the bougainvillea, the classical guitar on a hidden record player, and the adroitly placed lighting, together with the majesty of the rising of the evening stars, joined themselves with the magnificence of the architecture—located as we were just five degrees north of the Equator in the savannah just beyond the coast—to make everything seem enchanted. Of course we spoke of the Gardens of Granada and Cordova and of the entry to the Women's Quarter of the Lal Quila at Delhi and the Shalmar at Lahore. The Hall speciality, rainbow trout fried in batter and served with chips (french fries), did reduce me to giggling. He asked me whether Ibn Battuta had got lost in black Africa, and I asked where his much more enormous work on the whole corpus of medieval Arabic sources was going. He took patiently a gentle leg-pull about the imperative he seemed to carry in his heart, needing physically to visit places before he wrote about them. He took with a friendly smile the insinuation that he was an Uwaysi sufi who liked to wrap his head and go to sleep in a holy place and perhaps see a vision or dream a dream of the holy person.

Nearer to recent times I last saw him helping wth a marathon swim of the Sea of Galilee. As he led me towards the ferry, I reminded him of the Jataka story of how the Buddha refused to levitate or swim across the Ganges since a ferry was not available. He told me I must not fail on the other shore to buy a St. Peter trout in honor of our meal at Legon, adding, "If there is a coin in its mouth do not doubt that it will go to fulfill your tax obligation to the imperial power." He was a colossus of enormous learning who could stride with detailed knowledge of Judaism, Christianity, and Islam. It is with awe and gratitude that we offer our studies in his memory and give thanks for the honor it is to include extracts from his books.

Publisher's Note

Professor Levtzion knew the publisher, Markus Wiener, personally very well, and told him time and again that it was his wish to make the texts he and J.F.P. Hopkins discovered and published in the *Corpus of Early Arabic Sources for West African History* as widely known as possible. He therefore included substantial parts in the book *Medieval West Africa,* which he edited together with Jay Spaulding, and for the same reason we have included the following excerpts in the present volume.

PRELIMINARY VISITS TO BLACK AFRICA—A SUMMARY

Ibn Baṭṭūṭa was a young man when he made his first visit to black Africa. In 726 A.H./A.D. 1326, he was in Egypt and wanted to go to Mecca. He went up the Nile to Luxor in southern Egypt, across the Nile at Adfū and thence across the desert for fifteen days to the town of ʿAidhāb on the African side of the Red Sea. He found that the people were Bujā (Beja), black in colour, wearing yellow robes with head-ties about a finger's width wide. They did not permit their daughters to inherit. The town belonged two-thirds to their king and one-third to the king of Egypt. At that town he visited a mosque rich in *baraka* and a venerable shaikh who claimed to be a son of a Moroccan king. He discovered that the mamlūk soldiers from Egypt had been defeated by the local sultan who had sunk the shipping. The journey across the Red Sea to Jeddah was impossible, so ibn Baṭṭūṭa had to sell his provisions and return to Cairo the same way he had come. The Nile was in flood so this part of the journey only took eight days. He hurried on to Syria and continued his travels. [I 109-111].

A few years later (730 A.H./A.D. 1329-1330) ibn Baṭṭūṭa set out from Judda (Jeddah) and sailed for two days. The weather then became rough and they were blown to an anchorage off the African coast called Ra's Dawā'ir which is between ʿAidhāb and the island of Sawākin. There he found a shelter of reeds made on the model of a mosque and ostrich shells full of water.

There was also a tide-race in which the people caught great fish just by putting in a cloth and holding it at both ends. Once again he met the Bujā (Beja) and travelled with them over a plain full of deer. They came upon an Arab encampment belonging to the Awlād Kāhil who have mixed with the Bujā. Then they went on to the island of Sawākin. Water had to be brought to it but it exported milk-products and some coarse grain to Mecca. The sultan of Sawākin was closely connected to the *amīrs* of Mecca through his father, but the island came to him through his mother's Bujā relations. [II 160-163]

Fom Sawākin, ibn Baṭṭūṭa went to Al-Yaman and found his way to ᶜAdan (Aden).

Two years later, ibn Baṭṭūṭa again visited this coast on his way from Mecca to India. He had tried to get a ship going directly from Jedda but when he failed to do so, he crossed over to the African side of the Red Sea, making for ᶜAidhāb. Unfortunately, he was driven by the wind to Ra's Dawā'ir and had to go overland nine days across very dry country before he reached ᶜAidhāb. The Bujā controlled the area, although there were also some Arabs there. An Arab youth who was a slave to the Bujā said that he had lived on camel's milk for a year. Ibn Baṭṭūṭa was able to hire camels and make his way on to the Nile and travel to Cairo [II 251-254].

From there he went to India by way of Asia Minor and southern Russia. He mentions without details that he passed ᶜAidhāb again in the reverse direction on his way to Mecca in 1348 after he had visited China [IV 324]. After this he returned home, visited Spain, and then set out on his last great journey to Malli, which is for him *the* land of the blacks.

Ibn Khaldun[1]

Ibn Khaldun is the best-known Arab historian. He was born in Tunis in 1332, and spent most of his life in the service of North African rulers. Toward the end of his life he moved to Egypt, where he died in 1406. His most famous work is the Introduction (al-muqaddima) *to his voluminous universal history. This work, known by its shorter title as* The Book of Examples (Kitab al-ʿibar), *was written in the years 1374–78; however, Ibn Khaldun continued to revise and update events in Mali until 1394.*

Ibn Khaldun is unique among the Arab authors in appreciating the value of historical traditions. He recorded the oral history of Mali from Shaykh ʿUthman, who visited Cairo in 1394. Ibn Khaldun was able to present a review of the history of the lands of the Sudan over a period of four centuries, from the hegemony of Ghana through the Almoravids' intervention and the interlude of the Susu (who are prominent in the oral traditions but do not appear in other Arab sources before Ibn Khaldun) to the rise of Mali. Other informants were al-Hajj Yunus, probably the resident translator for Mali in Cairo, and a qadi from Sijilmasa who had lived for many years in Kawkaw. Ibn Khaldun met him at Hunayn in Algeria in 1374–75. Ibn Khaldun was careful to ask his informants about the exact pronunciation of African names.

A critical analysis of Ibn Khaldun's text permits the following reconstruction of the genealogy of the kings of Mali:

1. Source: N. Levtzion and Jay Spaulding, *Medieval West Africa* (Princeton: Markus Wiener Publishers, 2003), pp. 89–101.

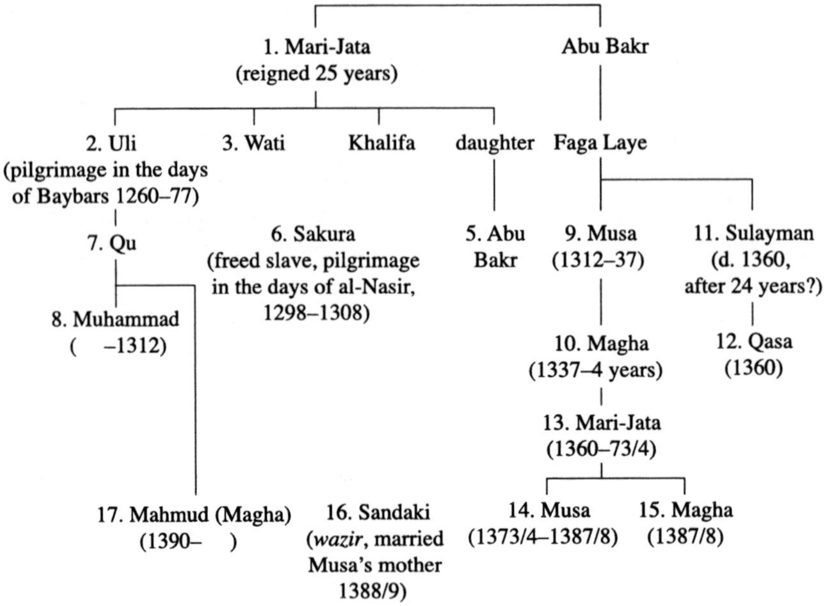

Ibn Khaldun's history gives an account of the exchange of diplomatic missions between Mali and Morocco. He was in Fez from 1354 to 1363, and witnessed himself the arrival there of the Malian mission during December 1360 or January 1361. He describes the excitement created by the gift of a giraffe that this mission brought to the Moroccan sultan.

THE PILGRIMAGE OF THE KING OF THE TAKRUR

....The first among them to do so was Barmandar [*sic*]. I have heard from some of their eminent men that they pronounce his name Barmandana. The kings after him followed his example in performing the Pilgrimage.

Then Mansa Wali the son of Mari Jata went on the Pilgrimage during the reign of [the Mamluk sultan] al-Zahir Baybars [1260--

77]. The next one among them on the Pilgrimage was Sakurah, their freed slave, who had usurped their kingship. It was he who conquered the town of Kawkaw. Then he went on the Pilgrimage during the [second] reign of [the Mamluk sultan] al-Nasir [1299–1309]. After him Mansa Musa made the Pilgrimage, as is recounted in their history in dealing with the Berber dynasties, in the account of the Sanhaja and the dynasty of the Lamtuna, one of their peoples.

When Mansa Musa left the land of the Maghrib for the Pilgrimage he followed the desert route, and came out near the Pyramids in Egypt. He sent a rich present to al-Nasir. It is said that it included 50,000 dinars. Al-Nasir accommodated him at al-Qarafa 'l-Kubra and gave it to him as a fief. The sultan received him in his audience room, talked to him, gave him a gift, and supplied him with provisions. He gave him horses and camels, and sent along with him emirs to serve him until he performed his religious duty in the year 724/1324. On his return journey in the Hijaz he was stricken by a disaster from which his fate rescued him. It so happened that on the way he strayed from the *mahmil* and the caravan and was left alone with his people away from the Arabs. This route was completely unknown to them, and they could not find the way to a settlement or come upon a watering place. They went towards the horizon until they came out at Suez. They were eating fish whenever they could find some and the bedouin were snatching up the stragglers until they were saved.

The sultan then again bestowed honors upon him and was generous in his gifts. It is said that he had prepared in his country for his expenses a hundred loads of gold, each load weighing three qintars. This was all exhausted, and he could not meet his expenses. He therefore borrowed money from the principal merchants. Among those merchants who were in his company were the Banu'l-Kuwayk, who gave him a loan of 50,000 *dinars*. He sold to them the palace that the sultan had bestowed on him as a gift. He [the sultan?] approved it. Siraj al-Din b. al-Kuwayk sent his agent along with him to collect what he had loaned to him but the agent died there. Siraj al-Din sent another [emissary] with his son. He [the emissary] died but the son, Fakhr al-Din Abu Jaʿfar, got back some of it. Mansa Musa died before he [Siraj al-Din?] died, so they obtained nothing [more] from him . . .

THE KINGS OF THE SUDAN; A DESCRIPTION OF THEIR CIRCUMSTANCES, AND A BRIEF SKETCH OF WHAT HAS COME TO OUR KNOWLEDGE CONCERNING THEIR DYNASTIES

When Ifriqiya and the Maghrib were conquered [by the Arabs] merchants penetrated the western part of the land of the Sudan and found among them no king greater than the king of Ghana. Ghana was bounded on the west by the ocean. They were a very mighty people exercising vast authority. The seat of their authority was Ghana, a dual city on both banks of the Nile, one of the greatest and most populous cities in the world. It is mentioned by the authors of the *Book of Roger* [al-Idrisi] and the *Book of Routes and Realms* [al-Bakri].

The neighbors of Ghana on the east, as chroniclers assert, were another people known as Susu [with the letter *sad*] or Susu [with the letter *sin*] and beyond them another people known as Mali, and beyond them another known as Kawkaw or Kaghu, then beyond them another known as Takrur. I learn from Shaykh ʿUthman, the *faqih* of the people of Ghana and one of their chief men, and the most learned, religious, and celebrated of them, whom I met when he came to Egypt in [7]96/1394 in the course of the Pilgrimage with his family, that they call the Takrur "Zaghay" and the Mali "Ankariya." Later the authority of the people of Ghana waned and their prestige declined as that of the veiled people, their neighbors on the north next to the land of the Berbers, grew (as we have related). These extended their domination over the Sudan, and pillaged, imposed tribute and the poll tax, and converted many of them to Islam. Then the authority of the rulers of Ghana dwindled away and they were overcome by the Susu, a neighboring people of the Sudan, who subjugated and absorbed them.

Later the people of Mali outnumbered the peoples of the Sudan in their neighborhood and dominated the whole region. They vanquished the Susu and acquired all their possessions, both their ancient kingdom and that of Ghana as far as the ocean on the west. They were Muslims. It is said that the first of them to embrace Islam was a king named Barmandana (thus vocalized by Shaykh ʿUthman), who made the Pilgrimage and was followed in this practice by the kings after him. Their greatest king, he who overcame the Susu, conquered their country, and seized the power from their hands, was named Mari Jata. *Mari*, in their language, means "ruler of the blood royal," and *jata* "lion." Their word for *hafid* ("servant" or "son-in-law") is TKN. I have not heard the genealogy of this king. He ruled for 25 years, according to what they relate, and when he died his son Mansa Wali ruled after him. In their language *mansa* means "sultan" and *wali* means "ʿAli." This Mansa Wali was one of their greatest kings. He made the Pilgrimage in the days of al-Zahir Baybars. His brother Wati ruled after him and then a third brother, Khalifa. Khalifa was insane and devoted to archery and used to shoot arrows at his people and kill them wantonly so they rose against him and killed him. A grandson of Mari Jata, called Abu Bakr, who was the son of his daughter, succeeded him. They made him king according to the custom of these non-Arabs, who bestow the kingship on the sister and the son of the sister [of a former king]. We do not know his or his father's pedigree.

Their next ruler was one of their clients who usurped their kingship. His name was Sakura, pronounced Sabkara by the people of Ghana in their language, according to Shaykh ʿUthman. Sakura performed the Pilgrimage during the reign of al-Malik al-Nasir and was killed while on the return journey at Tajura. During his mighty reign their dominions expanded and they overcame the neighboring peoples. He conquered the land of Kawkaw and brought it within the rule of the people of Mali. Their rule reached from the ocean and Ghana in the west to the land of Takrur [sic] in the east. Their authority became mighty and all the peoples of the Sudan stood in awe of them. Merchants from the Maghrib and Ifriqiya traveled to their country. Al-Hajj Yunus, the Takruri interpreter, said that the conqueror of Kawkaw was Saghmanja, one of the generals of Mansa Musa.

The ruler after this Sakura was Qu, grandson of the sultan Mari Jata, then after him his son Muhammad b. Qu. After him their kingship passed from the line of Mari Jata to that of his brother Abu Bakr in the person of Mansa Musa b. Abi Bakr. Mansa Musa was an upright man and a great king, and tales of his justice are still told. He made the Pilgrimage in 724/1324 and encountered during the ceremonies the Andalusian poet Abu Ishaq Ibrahim al-Sahili, known as al-Tuwayjin. Abu Ishaq accompanied Mansa Musa to his country and there enjoyed an esteem and consideration which his descendants have inherited after him and keep to this day. They are settled in Walatan on the western frontier of their country.

On his return journey Mansa Musa was met by our friend al-Muʿammar Abu ʿAbd Allah b. Khadija al-Kumi, a descendant of ʿAbd al-Mu'min [the Almohad ruler]. Muʿammar had been a propagandist in the Zab for the Expected Mahdi [the Almohad founder] and had made raids upon the inhabitants of the Zab with guerilla bands of Arabs. The ruler of Wargalan had captured him by a ruse but released him after a time and he set off through the wilderness to seek from Mansa Musa forces with which to avenge himself. Having heard that Mansa Musa had set off on the Pilgrimage he stayed to wait for him in the town of Ghadamis in the hope of obtaining help against his enemy and support for his mission because of the power of Mansa Musa's authority in the desert adjacent to the territory of Wargalan. Al-Muʿammar was well received and Mansa Musa promised him assistance in taking his revenge and invited him to accompany him to his country. Al-Muʿammar, a truthful man, told me: "We used to keep the sultan company during his progress, I and Abu Ishaq al-Tuwayjin, to the exclusion of his viziers and chief men, and converse to his enjoyment. At each halt he would regale us with rare foods and confectionery. His equipment and furnishings were carried by 12,000 private slave women wearing gowns of brocade and Yemeni silk."

According to al-Hajj Yunus, the interpreter for this nation at Cairo, this man Mansa Musa came from his country with 80 loads of gold dust, each load weighing three *qintar*s. In their own country they use only slave women and men for transport but for distant journeys such as the Pilgrimage they have mounts.

Ibn Khadija continues: "We returned with him to the capital of his kingdom. He wished to acquire a house as the seat of his authority, solidly constructed and clothed with plaster on account of its unfamiliarity in their land, so Abu Ishaq al-Tuwayjin made something novel for him by erecting a square building with a dome. He had a good knowledge of handicrafts and lavished all his skill on it. He plastered it over and covered it with colored patterns so that it turned out to be the most elegant of buildings. It caused the sultan great astonishment because of the ignorance of the art of building in their land and he rewarded Abu Ishaq for it with 12,000 *mithqal*s of gold dust apart from the preference, favor, and splendid gifts which he enjoyed."

There were diplomatic relations and exchanges of gifts between this sultan Mansa Musa and the contemporary Merinid king of the Maghrib, sultan Abu'l-Hasan. High-ranking statesmen of the two kingdoms were exchanged as ambassadors. The ruler of the Maghrib chose with care such products and novelties of his kingdom as people spoke of for long after (as will be mentioned in its place) and sent them by the hand of ʿAli b. Ghanim, the emir of the Maʿqil, and other dignitaries of his state. The successors of these two monarchs inherited these relations, as will be mentioned.

The reign of this Mansa Musa lasted for 25 years. On his death his son Mansa Magha succeeded him as ruler of Mali. Magha with them means "Muhammad." Mansa Magha died within four years of succeeding and was followed by Mansa Sulayman b. Abi

Bakr, who was Musa's brother. His reign lasted 24 years, then he died and his son Qasa b. Sulayman succeeded him only to die nine months after his succession. After him ruled Mari Jata b. Mansa Magha b. Mansa Musa, whose reign lasted fourteen years. He was a most wicked ruler over them because of the tortures, tyrannies, and improprieties to which he subjected them. In [7]62/1360-61 he presented to the king of the Maghrib at that time, the sultan Abu Salim son of sultan Abu'l-Hasan, the gifts which are often mentioned, among which was that huge creature which provoked astonishment in the Maghrib, known as the giraffe. The people talked of it for long because of the various adornments and markings that it combined in its body and attributes.

The trustworthy *qadi* Abu ʿAbd Allah Muhammad b. Wasul of Sijilmasa, who had settled in the land of Kawkaw in their country and had been employed as qadi there and whom I met at Hunayn in 776/1374-75, gave me a great deal of information about their kings which I wrote down. He told me about this sultan Jata, that he ruined their empire, squandered their treasure, and all but demolished the edifice of their rule. "His extravagance and prolifigacy," said Abu ʿAbd Allah, "reached such a point that he sold the boulder of gold which was a prized possession of their treasury. It was a boulder weighing twenty *qintar*s that had been transported from the mine without being worked or purified by fire. They regarded it as the rarest and most precious of treasures because its like is so scarce in the mines.

"Jata, this prolifigate king, offered it to the Egyptian traders who travel back and forth to his country, and they bought it at a derisory price. In his loose living he squandered other royal treasures. He was stricken by sleeping sickness, a disease that often afflicts the inhabitants of that region, particularly the aristocracy. The victim suffers from attacks of sleepiness at all times until he hardly awakes except for short intervals. The disease becomes chronic and the attacks are continuous until he dies. This Jata was afflicted by this disease for two years and died in [7]75/1373–74.

"They appointed his son Musa to succeed him. He adopted a way of justice and moderation towards his people and quite abandoned the way of his father. Nowadays his advice is sought, but his vizier Mari Jata has seized his authority. (*Mari*, in their language, means "vizier" and *jata* has been explained above.) Mari Jata holds the sultan in seclusion and has taken his power exclusively into his own hands. He has seen to the mobilization of the army and the gathering of the squadrons. He has subdued the eastern provinces of their country and passed beyond the frontiers of Kawkaw. When he first assumed authority he sent against Takedda (which is in the country of the veil-wearers beyond Kawkaw) detachments that laid siege to it and invested it closely but then let it be. That is their situation at present.

"This Takedda [actually Tadmekka] is 70 stages from the town of Wargala towards the southwest. Its chief, who is of the wearers of the veil, is known as the sultan. The route of the pilgrims of the Sudan passes through his territory. He exchanges gifts and maintains diplomatic relations with the emirs of Zab and Wargala.

"The capital of the people of Mali is the town of BNY, an extensive place with cultivated land fed by running water, very populous with brisk markets. At present it is a station for trading caravans from the Maghrib, Ifriqiya, and Egypt, and goods are imported from all parts."

We have just heard that Mansa Musa died in the year [7]89/1387 and that his brother Mansa Magha succeeded him. Mansa Magha was killed after a year or so and was succeeded by Sandaki, the husband of Musa's mother (*sandaki* means "vizier"), but after a few months he was assassinated by a member of Mari Jata's family. Then there came forth from the land of the pagans beyond them a man named Mahmud, related to Mansa Qu b. Mansa Wali b. Mari Jata the Great, who seized power and became ruler in [7]92/1390. His title is Mansa Magha . . . .

In the year [6]55/1257 there arrived [at Tunis, the Hafsid capital] gifts from the king of Kanim, one of the kings of the Sudan, ruler of Borno, whose domains lie to the south of Tripoli. Among them was a giraffe, an animal of strange form and incongruous characteristics . . . .

At a distance of twenty stages slightly to the west and south of this city [Wargala] is Takedda [Tadmekka], the capital of the veiled men's country and rendezvous for pilgrims of the Sudan. It was founded by veiled men of Sanhaja, who are its inhabitants at the present day. Its ruler is an emir of one of their leading houses and they call him sultan. There are diplomatic relations and exchanges of gifts between him and the emir of the Zab.

In the year [7]54/1353, in the days of sultan Abu 'Inan [of Morocco], I went to Biskara on royal business and there encountered the ambassador of the ruler of Takedda at the residence of Yusuf al-Muzani, emir of Biskara. He told me about the prosperous state of this city and the continual passage of wayfarers and said: "This year there passed through our city on the way to Mali a caravan of merchants from the east containing 12,000 camels." Another [informant] has told me that this is a yearly event. This country is subject to the sultan of Mali of the Sudan as is the case at present with the rest of the desert regions known as [the land of] the veiled men . . . .

[Hilal, chamberlain of Abu Tashfin, ruler of Tlemcen, went on the Pilgrimage.] He set sail in [7]24/1324 and disembarked at Alexandria. He went with the Pilgrims from Egypt in the party of the Commander [of the Caravan]. On the way he met the sultan of the Sudan from Mali, Mansa Musa, and a firm friendship grew up between them . . . .

THE SULTAN'S GIFT TO THE KING OF MALI OF THE SUDAN BORDERING ON THE MAGHRIB

Sultan Abu'l-Hasan was well known for his ostentatious ways and his presumption to vie with the mightiest monarchs and adopt their customs in exchanging gifts with their peers and counterparts and dispatching emissaries to distant kings and far frontiers. In his time the king of Mali was the greatest of the kings of the Sudan and the nearest to his kingdom in the Maghrib. Mali was 100 stages distant over desert from the southern frontiers of his realms.

When Abu'l-Hasan took Tlemcen from the Banu ʿAbd al-Wad in 737/1337, seized their authority, and conquered the realms of the central Maghrib, people talked of the affair of the beleaguering and death of Abu Tashfin [ruler of Tlemcen] and of the aggressiveness of the sultan and his contempt of the enemy and the news spread through all lands. So sultan Mansa Musa of Mali (who has been mentioned above in the appropriate section) aspired to correspond with him. Accordingly he deputed some of his subjects to go as emissaries with an interpreter drawn from the veiled men of Sanhaja who are the neighbors of his kingdom. They presented themselves before the sultan and congratulated him on his victory over his enemies. Abu'l-Hasan received them with honor, lodged them well, and sent them away fittingly. Desirous of displaying his customary opulence, he chose from his household treasury the rarest and most magnificent objects of Maghribi manufacture and appointed several of his courtiers, including the secretary of chancellery Abu Talib b. Muhammad b. Abu Madyan and his freedman ʿAnbar the eunuch to convey them to the king of Mali [who was by then] Mansa Sulayman son [actually, the brother] of Mansa Musa, because his father [brother] had died before the return of his deputation. He also ordered certain of the desert Arabs of the Maʿqil to travel with them in both directions and this duty was undertaken by ʿAli b. Ghanim, emir of the Awlad Jar Allah of the Maʿqil, who accompanied them on their way in obedience to the sultan's command. This cortege set off across the desert and reached Mali after much effort and long privation. The king received them with honor and cordiality and dismissed them honorably. They returned to the one who had sent them accompanied by a deputation of Mali grandees who lauded his authority, acknowledged his rights, and conveyed to him that with which their master had charged them, namely [the expression of] humble submission and readiness to pay the sultan his due and act in accordance with his wishes.

Their mission being carried out, the sultan had achieved his aim of vaunting himself over other kings and exacting their submission to his authority and so he fulfilled God's due of thanks for His favor . . . .

[In 749/1348–49, following the conquest of Ifriqiya by Abu'l

Hasan, several deputations converged on Constantine.] Among them also was a delegation from the people of Mali, kings of the Sudan in the Maghrib, who had been sent by their king Mansa Sulayman to offer congratulations on the dominion over Ifriqiya ....

THE DEPUTATION OF THE SUDAN, THEIR GIFT, AND THE AMAZEMENT THAT THEY PROVOKED WITH A GIRAFFE

When sultan Abu'l-Hasan sent to the king of the Sudan, Mansa Sulayman son of Mansa Musa, the gift which has been mentioned in its place, Mansa Sulayman occupied himself in preparing a comparable gift For this purpose he collected wonderful and strange objects of his country. Meanwhile Abu'l-Hasan died [in 752/1351] and by the time the gift had reached the furthest outpost of Mali at Walatan Mansa Sulayman had died [also about 760/1358–59].

Dissension now broke out among the people of Mali. Authority over them became divided and their [rival] kings tried to seize power. They killed each other and were preoccupied with civil war until finally Mansa Jata emerged and consolidated power in his hands. Examining the regions of his empire, he was told of the circumstances of this gift and was informed that it was at Walatan. He ordered it to be sent on to the king of the Maghrib and added to it a giraffe, a strangely-shaped and large-framed creature resembling various other animals.

They departed from their country and reached Fez in Safar [7]62/December 1360–January 1361. The day of their arrival was a memorable one. The sultan sat to receive them in the Golden Tower as he would for a review and criers summoned the people to go out to the open space outside the city. They came out, "hastening out of every mound" [Koran 21:36] until the space was too small for them and they climbed upon each other in the press round the giraffe in amazement at its form. The poets recited poems of eulogy and congratulation and description of the scene.

The deputation presented themselves before the sultan and delivered their messages affirming the affection and sincere friendship [of their king], apologizing for the slow arrival of the gift because of the dissension among the people of Mali and their struggle for power, praising their sultan and the state of their realm. During all this the interpreter was translating for them and they were twanging their bowstrings in approbation according to their approved custom. They greeted the sultan by scattering dust on their heads in conformity with the custom of non-Arab kings.

Then the king remounted and the assembly dispersed. Talk of it became widespread. The deputation continued to be entertained by the sultan, who died before their departure. His successor [Abu ʿUmar Tashfin, who succeeded in 1361], however, continued to give them hospitality until they departed for Marrakech and from there passed on to the territory of the Dhawi Hassan, Maʿqil Arabs who inhabit the [desert to the south of the] Sus and whose territory marches with that of the Sudan. And from there they rejoined their sultan.

Al-Khabar 'an ajnas al-Sudan, attributed to al-Maqrizi[2]

A fragment entitled "An Epistle on the Races of the Sudan," attributed to al-Maqrizi, was edited by Hamaker in 1820. It includes important information about Kanim and Borno. The latest date in this text is the year 800/1397–98. When this information is collated with data provided by Ibn Battuta and al-Qalqashandi it is possible to reconstruct a genealogy of the kings of the Saifawa dynasty of Kanim-Borno over the three generations that cover the whole of the fourteenth century.

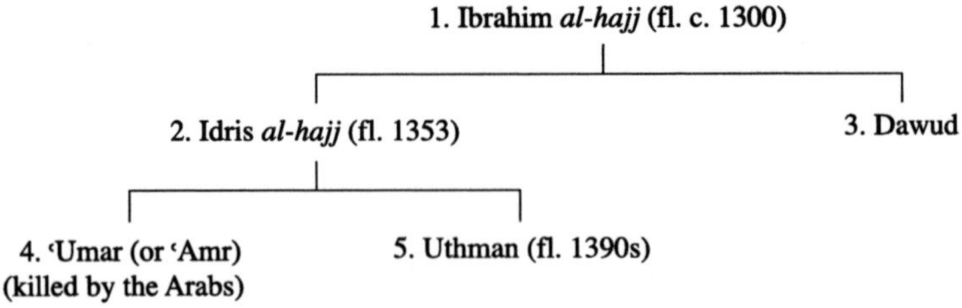

According to the sixteenth-century chronicle of Ibn Furtu, Kanim was abandoned during the reign of Dawud b. Ibrahim (about 1366–76). According to the Diwan Salatin Burnu *it was during the reign of 'Umar b. Idris (about 1382–87). According to the letter copied by al-Qalqashandi, the Judham Arabs killed 'Umar.*

THE RACES OF THE SUDAN

. . . [The Kanim are a numerous] people among whom Islam predominates. Their city is Aljama. The first of their kings to adopt Islam was Muhammad b. Jabal b. 'Abd Allah b. 'Uthman b.

2. Source: N. Levtzion and Jay Spaulding, *Medieval West Africa* (Princeton: Markus Wiener Publishers, 2003), pp. 107–108.

Muhammad b. ʿBY——. They assert that he is descended from Sayf b. Dhi Yazan and that between the two there were about 40 kings. This king is a wandering bedouin. When he sits on his throne his subjects make obeisance to him and fall on their faces. His armies, including cavalry, infantry, and porters, number 100,000. Between Aljama and Yalamlam there dwell many unbelievers. The king of Aljama, i.e. the king of Kanim, has five [minor] kings under his sway. Their horses are small. Kanim is a vast region through which the blessed Nile flows . . . .

Their king in about 700/1300 was al-Hajj Ibrahim of the posterity of Sayf b. Dhi Yazan. He held the throne of Kanim. Kanim is the throne of Borno. There ruled after him his son al-Hajj Idris, then his brother Daʾud b. Ibrahim, then ʿUmar the son of his brother al-Hajj Idris, then his brother ʿUthman b. Idris who ruled a little before 800/1397-98. The people of Kanim then rose against them and apostatized and . . . . They are Muslims and wage Holy War on the people of Kanim. They have twelve kingdoms.

Al-Maqqari[3]

Al-Maqqari was born in Tlemcen ca. 1591–92 and died in Cairo in 1632. His Nafh al-Tib *is a compilation of historical and biographical material from earlier sources related to Muslim Spain. The text quoted below includes three contemporary accounts from the fourteenth century concerning the Andalusian architect who accompanied Mansa Musa back to Mali and died at Timbuktu.*

[CHAPTER V: ON THOSE ANDALUSIANS
WHO TRAVELED TO THE EAST]

"Among them was Abu Ishaq al-Sahili, known as al-Tuwayjin or al-Tuwayjan, the celebrated scholar, the upright man for whom thanks are given, the renowned poet, a native of Granada from a family of rectitude, wealth, and trust. His father was the head of the perfumers' guild in Granada. As well as being head [of the guild] he was a scholar and lawyer, proficient and versatile. He was well versed in the law of inheritance.

"In his youth this Abu Ishaq was a notary in the lawyers' street of Granada. He departed from al-Andalus for the East and made the Pilgrimage and then travelled to the land of the Sudan. He made his home there and found high favor with its sultan. He died there, may God have mercy upon him." Here ends a summary of the words of the emir Ibn al-Ahmar in his book, *Nathir al-Juman fi man nazamani wa-iyyahu al-zaman*.

3. Source: N. Levtzion and Jay Spaulding, *Medieval West Africa* (Princeton: Markus Wiener Publishers, 2003), pp. 109–10.

Abu'l-Makarim Mindil b.Ajurrum said:"It was related to me by one whose words may be trusted that the death of Abu Ishaq al-Tuwayjin took place on Monday 27 Jumada II 745/15 October 1346 at Tunbuktu, a place in the desert which is one of the provinces of Mali, may God have mercy on him."Then he vocalized al-Tuwayjin with "i" after the "j" and said: "This is how he vocalized it with his own hand, may God have mercy on him. Those who call him al-Sahili name him after his maternal grandfather."

Among them was the excellent imam, the litterateur Abu Ishaq Ibrahim b. Muhammad al-Sahili al-Gharnati. Al-ʿIzz b. Jamaʿa [the Shafiʿi *qadi* of Cairo, d. 1366] says: "He came to us from the Maghrib in the year 724/1324 then returned to the Maghrib in that year. We have heard that he died at Marrakech in the 740s/1340s."

Mali became known in Egypt through the spectacular visit to Cairo of Mansa Musa on his way to and from Mecca. So impressive was this visit that it was recorded as one of the major events of the year 724/1324 by Egyptian chroniclers of the fourteenth and fifteenth centuries. These historians recorded also other Takruri pilgrims.

Ibn al-Dawadari[4]

Ibn al-Dawadari wrote the history of the Muslim dynasties in nine volumes between 1331 and 1335, that is, he wrote less than ten years after Mansa Musa's visit to Cairo. He obtained some details about the kingdom of Mali from informants whom he mentions by name. This information should be compared with that of his contemporary al-ʿUmari. Ibn al-Dawadari has two pieces of information of political significance. One is that the ʿAbbasid caliph, who was resident in Cairo as a puppet of the Mamluk sultans, girded Mansa Musa with a sword. In later years the Tarikhs *of Timbuktu would have similar accounts concerning Askiya Muhammad of Songhay, that the ʿAbbasid Caliph girded him with a sword, when he visited Cairo at the end of the fifteenth century. The second piece of information, which is unconfirmed by any other source, is that Mansa Musa undertook that the* khutba *(sermon) and the coinage in Mali would be in the name of the Mamluk sultan. Both are signs of formal political submission to a sovereign.*

4. Source: N. Levtzion and Jay Spaulding, *Medieval West Africa* (Princeton: Markus Wiener Publishers, 2003), pp. 111–13.

In this year 724/1324 the king of the Takrur arrived making for the Noble Hijaz. His name was Abu Bakr b. Musa [elsewhere Musa b.Abu Bakr]. He remained in Egypt for a year before betaking himself to the Hijaz. He had much gold with him. His is the country that puts forth gold.

I heard the *qadi* Fakhr al-Din, Inspector of the (victorious) Army say: "I asked the king of the Takrur: 'How is the description of the place where the gold grows with you?' He replied: 'It is not in that part of our land which belongs to the Muslims, but in the land which belongs to the Christians [*sic*] of the Takrur. We dispatch [collectors] to take from them a species of tribute due to us and obligatory upon them. These are special lands which put forth gold in this fashion: it consists of small pieces of varying sizes, some like little rings, some like carob seeds, and the like.'"

The *qadi* Fakhr al-Din continued: "I said: 'Why don't you take this land by conquest?' He replied: 'If we conquer them and take it, it does not put forth anything. We have done this in many ways but seen nothing there; but when it returns to them it puts forth as usual. This is a most amazing thing and is perhaps due to an increase in the oppressiveness of the Christians.'"

Then the king of the Takrur and his followers bought all kinds of things from New and Old Cairo. They thought that their money was inexhaustible. When they became immersed in buying and found that there was no limit to the different commodities in this country and they saw every day something better than the last, the money that they had with them gave out and they needed to borrow. Avaricious people lent to them in the hope of big profits on their return, but everything they had borrowed fell back on the heads of the lenders and they got nothing back. Among these was our friend the *shaykh* and *imam* Shams al-Din b.Tazmart al-Maghribi. He lent them gold of good form but none of it came back.Then these people became amazed at the ampleness of this country and how their money had been used up without their having been able to complete the purchases they desired. So they became needy and resold what they had bought at half its value, and people made good profits out of them. And God knows best.

Our lord was very generous towards them and invested the king with a royal robe of honor by his authority, while the caliph girded him with a sword by his authority. He undertook that the *khutba* in his country should be in the name of our lord the sultan and the coinage likewise. Such an undertaking was never given to a ruler of Egypt except our lord the sultan [al-Nasir] (may his victories be mighty).

Al-Maqrizi[5]

Al-Maqrizi (1364–1442) was one of the most famous historians of the Mamluk period. He studied with Ibn Khaldun when the latter was resident in Cairo in the years 1382–1406. The texts below are drawn from three different works by al-Maqrizi. The first text is a detailed account of Mansa Musa in a treatise devoted to kings who made the Pilgrimage. The second is from al-Maqrizi's work on the topography of Cairo, in which he refers also to a madrasa *endowed in the middle of the thirteenth century for the use of pilgrims from Kanim. The third text is from al-Maqrizi's annals, in which events are recorded in sequence. There are three references to the pilgrimage in the year* **724/1324**; *Mansa Musa arrived in Cairo on 19 July, the pilgrims' caravan which he joined departed three months later on 18 October, and it returned on 27 December. There are at least five additional entries referring to pilgrims from West Africa (Takrur). On two occasions there was a king in the pilgrims' caravans. All the pilgrims' caravans brought slaves and gold.*

THE KINGS OF THE TAKRUR WHO MADE THE PILGRIMAGE:
MANSA MUSA, KING OF THE TAKRUR

The first of the kings of the Takrur to make the Pilgrimage was Sarabandana or Baramandana. Then Mansa Wali son of Mari Jata did so in the days of al-Malik al-Zahir Baybars; then Sakura, who had usurped their throne and conquered the land of Kawkaw; then Mansa Musa.

Mansa Musa arrived in Egypt in 724/1324 with magnificent gifts and much gold. The sultan al-Malik al-Nasir b. Qalawun sent

5. Source: N. Levtzion and Jay Spaulding, *Medieval West Africa* (Princeton: Markus Wiener Publishers, 2003), pp. 115–18.

the *mihmandar* to receive him and Musa rode to the Citadel on the day of his official reception. He refused to kiss the ground and said to the interpreter: "I am a man of the Maliki school and do not prostrate myself before any but God." So the sultan excused him and drew him near to him and did him honor. The sultan asked him the reason for his coming and he replied: "I wish to make the Pilgrimage." So the sultan ordered the *wazir* to equip him with everything he might need.

It is said that he brought with him 14,000 slave girls for his personal service. The members of his entourage proceeded to buy Turkish and Ethiopian slave girls, singing girls, and garments, so that the rate of the gold *dinar* fell by six *dirhams*. Having presented his gift he set off with the caravan. The sultan had committed him to the care of the emir Sayf al-Din Itmish, commander of the caravan, and he [and his companions] traveled as a self-contained company in the rear of the pilgrim caravan. When he had completed his Pilgrimage he remained behind for several days at Mecca after the ceremonies. Then he turned back but many of his followers and camels perished from cold so that only about a third of them arrived with him. Consequently he needed to borrow much money from the merchants. He bought several books on Maliki jurisprudence. The sultan presented him with horses and camels and he set off for his own country, having given away much wealth as alms in the two holy cities. Whenever his companions addressed him on any subject they bared their heads while speaking to him, according to a custom of theirs.

AL-MAQRIZI, KITAB AL-MAWA'IZ

The *madrasa* of Ibn Rashiq. This *madrasa* belongs to the Malikis and is situated in the Hammam al-Rish quarter in Old Cairo. When the [people of] Kanim (one of the communities of the Takrur) reached Cairo in the 640s/1240s proposing to make the Pilgrimage they paid to the *qadi* 'Alam al-Din Ibn Rashiq money with which he built it. He taught there and so it took its name from him. It acquired a great reputation in the land of the Takrur and in most years they used to send money to it.

AL-MAQRIZI, KITAB AL-SULUK

[In 724/1324] Mansa Musa, king of Takrur, arrived proposing to make the Pilgrimage. He stayed for three days beneath the Pyramids as an official guest. He crossed to the Cairo bank on Thursday 26 Rajab [19 July 1324] and went up to the Citadel [to pay his respects to the sultan]. He declined to kiss the ground and was not forced to do so though he was not enabled to sit in the royal presence. The sultan commanded that he be equipped for the Pilgrimage. Then he came down. He paid out so much gold in buying what he desired in the way of slave girls, garments and other things that the rate of the dinar fell by six *dirhams* ....

On Tuesday 28 [Shawwal 724/18 October 1324] the caravan departed from Birkat al-Hajj for the Hijaz ....

On Friday 10 [Muharram 725/27 December 1324] the first pilgrims arrived [back from the Pilgrimage] ... On Saturday the 25th the *mahmil* and the remainder of the pilgrims arrived with the emir Itmish al-Muhammadi, commander of the caravan . . . .

On 20 [Ramadan 744/5 February 1344] the pilgrims' *mahmil* set off from al-Birka. More than 10,000 Maghribi pilgrims had come and about 5,000 from the land of Takrur . . . .

On 15 [Shawwal 752/5 December 1351] the pilgrims' *mahmil* set off . . . A great company of people of the Maghrib had come, and also the Takrur, having many slaves with them, and among them was their king . . . .

During this month [Shawwal 819/November–December 1416] the caravan of the Takrur arrived to perform the Pilgrimage. They had with them 1,700 head of men and women slaves and a great deal of gold dust . . . .

In this year [835/1431–32] one of the kings of the Takrur arrived to perform the Pilgrimage. He travelled to al-Tur, there to embark for Mecca, but died at al-Tur and was buried in the mosque there. He was an upright man who recited the Koran frequently and had charity and kindness . . . .

During this month [Shawwal 842/March–April 1439] the caravan of the Takrur arrived with many slaves as well as gold dust. Most of them went to perform the Pilgrimage, having sold the slaves. Most of the slaves perished in the possession of those who bought them.

APPENDIX II
EAST AFRICA

RUINS OF A SULTAN'S PALACE AT AN EAST AFRICAN COASTAL CITY STATE
(14TH CENTURY)

Selections from
*The Customs of the Swahili People (Desturi Za Waswahili) of Mtoro Bin Mwinyi Bakari**

Mtoro Bin Mwinyi Bakari—Mtoro signifying some kind of runaway or a nickname for an escaper, either from evil or dangers—came from the family of a minor aristocrat (hence the Mwinyi) and was described in his day as a pure Swahili person. He went to Mosque school at Bagamoyo. (This was the town that grew up at the end of the safari trails which had led off across Africa to the Great Lakes and beyond. Dhows from its roadstead plied to Zanzibar and onwards to Hydramaut in southeast Arabia, and to the Persian or Arab Gulf.) There he also pursued Ilmu (higher Islamic studies beyond a thorough grounding in the Qur'ān) and was sometimes sent to preach the Friday sermon at the congregational Mosque. He seems to have taken employment with the incoming German imperial power, and he did so well that he was sent to Berlin to be lektor at the Seminar for Oriental Studies. He became close friends with Dr. Karl Velten, who encouraged him to write down the traditions and customs of his people. He also taught young German officers the elements of Arabic. He married a German lady and settled down in Germany, but was ordered back to East Africa. When the Germans in Tanganyika objected to a local person having a European wife, Mtoro and his wife went back to Germany, where he ended his days. Truly this man was able to take the three heaven-vaulting strides of Hindu mythology. He was a true lover of basic African life and tradition, and a scholar of Islam fully at home in things European. Some selections from the Customs of the Swahili *with regard to dancing are given here, but it is hoped they will stimulate the reader to read the book in full.*

Note also that it is written in a beautiful, gripping prose and comes to us in the Roman script. Up until about those times when the European powers were breaking in and scrabbling for Africa, there was a considerable literature in Swahili in the Arabic letters, presumably all of it in poetic form. Perhaps a number of the great epic poems (tendi) were written by women; certainly grandmothers have remained until our own day some of their most careful and appreciative guardians.

* The Desturi with notes was brought together to be published by the University of California Press, Berkeley and Los Angeles, 1981, under Mtoro's name. A revised text and a translation had been drawn up by J.W.T. Allen based on the two works published by Doctor Karl Velten, *Desturi za wasuaheli na khabari za desturi za sheri'a za wasuaheli* and *Sitten und Gebraueche der Suaheli*, Vandenhöck and Ruprecht, Göttingen, 1903, and handed over to N.Q. King to complete. Mr. Allen passed away in 1974. He was descended from the great Roland Allen, and from Colonel Tarleton, whose bad behavior toward the Americans who had revolted against the crown inspired Mr. Allen to a life of serving the local people in East Africa. He also served in the Sudan and Arabia. His wife was a great promoter of girls' schools in East Africa and was well remembered by the grandmothers in Tanga.

Of Dances for Enjoyment

OF ANCIENT DANCES

From ancient times the greatest expression of joy at weddings or on other occasions is the dance. If there is rivalry, they dance. All love the dance, the very old and the young. Even jumbes dance, for everybody loves it.

THE GREAT DANCE (OR THE BIG DRUM)

It is originally the dance of chieftancy. For it two drums are placed on beds in the yard and beaten with two sticks. The drummer, unless he is a jumbe, bares his head and feet, and the piper, if he is a slave, has bare feet, and the horn player too; but a freeman retains his cap.[1]

After these drums the third great drum is set up on a log. It is called *mkuwiro,* and it is the most important of the great drums. When these drums are beaten, the people dance, two at a time. They must be freemen: it is not the custom for slaves to dance the great dance. When the freemen dance, they bare their heads and feet.[2] When jumbes dance, they do not bare their heads or feet. A shaha or waziri dancing with a jumbe takes off his turban but not his cap. The dancers hold swords in their hands and dance with them, and when a jumbe dances he has two attendant slave girls, who circle with him. This dance has no songs.

The most common competitive dance in the past was the sendemre.[3] For this a big drum is placed in the yard with two *cbopuo,* a mrungura, a pipe, and a metal tray.[4] The big drum is set in the fork of a tree and beaten with two wooden sticks.The piper has a platform built for him in a tree. It is made of mats in the shape of a house. He has a bed made for him up there and a shade of betel branches. He plays and sings, and the people below respond with words such as:

We were together; now we are apart.
You eat from wooden platters; you have no plates at home.
Let us sew the Mtondoo people in a sack and throw it in the
sea.

or:

The Sitirihali folk are slaves; let us use them as slaves.
No very sick person can meet with the Prophet.

or:

Do not incite me to sing,Amri, or you will cry.
Your brother has built a house And runoffto Unyanyembe.[5]

In the dance the men hold swords, machetes, or walking sticks,and the women dance holding bunches of betel,and they dance round the yard.Then a man steps out of line and confronts a woman, and they dance together.This dance used to be danced on high days or wedding days or for fun or for competitions; but it is danced no more.

OF COMPETITIONS

In the old days there were on the coast many competitions.[6] For this they said, "Let us form a society of one quarter of the town to challenge another." They chose their leader, a vizier, a counselor, and a messenger. All affairs were referred to the leader—if a man died, or was going to be married, or was bereaved, the leader took charge. The vizier's business was that if any matter arose in the town, it was referred to the vizier, and he reported to the leader. The counselor was consulted on every matter, and the messenger summoned the people, going to every house to tell them, "Tomorrow there is a meeting at the leader's at nine o'clock, because somebody is dead," or "We are going to a funeral," or "We are going to condole." Then the society acted as one man. If anything happened to displease the leader, all followed his instructions, and if at a party somebody annoyed the leader, the party broke up.

In their dance competitions they danced all night for six or seven nights of continuous dancing. They spent a great deal of money, because if one society killed two goats, the other would kill four. On the last night of the dance there was a party, and the visitors and the local people were told. Every house made buns, and from every house were sent three *pishi* of rice and one of wheat flour and butter and sugar.[7] If not, one house was in disgrace.

The song of the competitors is:

Mr. So-and-so, stop your gossip,

The wedding is tomorrow and the fungate next day.
You will be bankrupt; leave Gongoni alone.[8]

and the other society sings:

We ask for peace for the water to flow,
For the *kolekole* and the *kowana* to hide.
Do not pass where the enemy is.[9]

This is an account of the competitions; but now they do this less than in the past, for "empty hands are not licked if they hold not a single grain."

THE *CHANDO* DANCE

There are set up one chapuo (double-ended drum), one *vumi* (also a drum, but upright), a *mganda,* and a pipe. It is performed in the yard by both men and women. They kneel down to dance, and they sing:

Chando is indeed a dance [for adults],
How can you, a little girl, wander about at night?
Chando is indeed a dance.

or:

We have come with the children to light a fire.
We have come with the children to light a fire.
The people of the house are asleep, not awake.
Open the door for me to come in.

THE *KIGOMA* DANCE

Originally this dance was held at weddings or just for fun. To it were invited men and women. When the women know that today there will be a kigoma, they get ready their best clothes and scent themselves. To perform the dance they use a house with a large outer room. The women stay on the roof with buffalo horns, and the men stay downstairs. One is the singer, called the *sogora,* two play the chapuo, one a vumi, and one a tray and one a pipe.

When the dance starts, the young men come out in their best clothes, with handkerchiefs in their hands. The sogora sings, "Here we are, here we are, you." Then two of the young men dance, and when they are tired two others relieve them. When the women see the men dancing, they trill on the roof, and they tie in a cloth chains or bracelets or rings to give to the dancers as their reward. Then the leader sings:

So-and-so, son of so-and-so,
Is dancing with his best friend.

and the men and women reply:

Yoo yoo, sir, yoo yoo, sir,
He is dancing with his brother.

or:

Sleep, sir, sleep.
Where you slept yesterday, sleep there today.

or:

Like you, like you, like you, hee.
Like you, like you, like you, hee.
We shall get another as good as you.[10]

or:

The way of the monitor lizard, the monitor lizard's way,
Everywhere he goes, the monitor lizard's way,
The way of the monitor lizard.

Finally at the end of the dance the rewards given by the women to the men are returned to the women. Those who have them ask, "Whose is this chain?" or "Whose is this ring?" The woman who owns it recognizes it and comes to take it. If the man likes the owner of the chain, he makes an arrangement with her and they become friends. But the flowers fastened to the clothes and called posies are taken by the men. They are made with cardamom and basil and treated with sweet oils. The kigoma is danced for three to seven days. There is no feasting, and the dancing starts in the afternoon or evening.

THE *TINGE* DANCE

This comes from inland. It is danced by men only and consists of buffeting each other without any drums. They arrange themselves in two rows, one on this side and one on that. They stamp with the right foot and then suddenly raise the right foot.

If one raises and lowers it quickly and the other is too slow, he is captured and joins the other side. They sing:

Who comes will be beaten—you,
Who comes will be beaten.

or:

The porpoise diving and coming up.

or:

Friend, O friend,
Move a leg, friend.

or:

The tomato plant grows where you plant it.

or:

Who goes to Pemba, who goes to Pemba,
Greet Mbaruk from Somanga.[11]

or:

Here is one, here is another,
The tinge player is quiet.
Here are two and another two,

The tinge player is quiet.
Here are three and another three,
The tinge player is quiet.
Here are four and another four,
The tinge player is quiet.

and so on up to ten. Then they sing, "Here is none, and here is none." They cheer over the beaten side, saying, "You are tired, you are tired." All respond, and they go on playing until they are tired.

THE *KIUMBIZI* DANCE

This is in the form of a fight. They play the chapuo, the vumi, the *upatu* (a sheet of metal beaten with a switch), and the pipe. The dance starts at 4 P.M. and goes on until midnight. It is danced under a tree that gives good shade, such as a mango. The young men come dressed in their best kanzu, (shirt almost down to the ankle), and the piper plays:

Come, devil, come, devil,
We will whitewash him.

The young men throw their sticks to each other, meaning that one is inviting another to dance with him. They dance with the sticks, and at first they dance properly with gestures, the sticks clashing together with no ill will; but if one is dancing with one whom he dislikes, for taking his wife or some long-standing disagreement, their enmity comes out in the kiumbizi.

When they wish to break off such a kiumbizi at sundown, they play a *bondogea* roll, and they play with thin sticks and dance with them. Thin sticks are given to children to learn the kiumbizi, and men use them for dancing with children.

The kiumbizi is now danced at weddings; but in old days it was danced at any time.

THE *KIDATU* OR *MSOMA* DANCE

This is danced by young women, *vigori* (maidens), *wari* (initiators), and married women.[12] It is danced at night, and it is danced in the yard, and the men come to watch. The women clap and sing:

Leave me, leave me, Ramadhani, leave me,
Do not strip the whole tree, For a piece of jackfruit.[13]

or:

Learning, you read learning,
The Qur'ān with jealousy is not Islam.[14]

or:

When a kigori is pregnant, She is partly a mwari—partly.[15]

or:

She moaned, ah, she moaned,
I am still but a mwari—and she moaned like a cow.

or:

Leave off and take me again,
Leave off and take me again.
To be seduced is bitter.[16]

or:

Not home, not home, Mkwaja is not home.
You eat your grain, and I will eat my yeast.[17]

Of Spirits

The Swahili, both men and women, hold polytheistic beliefs in male and female spirits.[1,2] If a woman has a three-day fever, she attributes to herself a spirit in need of reduction, especially if there is something wrong with her husband.[3] Her sickness becomes worse daily, and she does not leave her bed. When the parents see that their child is sick, they say, "Your wife has inherited her grandmother's spirit, and that is what is making her ill. When she was small we raised to her head the spirit of her grandmother, saying, 'Take care of this child until she grows up, and then we will give you your platter.[4] Now her grandmother is dead, and her spirit demands its platter and has possessed its grandchild." If the husband does not attend to the words of his parents-in-law, people are offended with him and say that he is mean. They call him the one who has swallowed iron. But if he agrees with them that his wife has a *pepo* and that there must be a reduction, her parents are pleased and say that their daughter has a loving husband, and the woman agrees that he is a loving husband. He calls in a doctor to consult the omens, asking what is causing his wife's illness.

"There is nothing more than a spirit."

"Will you treat her?"

"First we must uncover the pot for her to see what is her condition."

There are two sorts of "pot"—stones and steam.

For the pot of stones, "queen bread" is dug up. This is the fungus grown in white-ant hills. Seven lumps are dug out and set on fire, for this stuff is inflammable. A matting hut is built, and the sick person comes and sits on a stool. A hole is dug, and a pot of water is brought. Her face is covered, and the lumps are quenched in the water in the hole. She inhales the steam and breaks into a sweat. That is the stone pot.

The steam pot is made by plucking leaves that will steam and putting them to cook in a pot. The patient leans over the steam and breaks into a sweat, and with more of the steaming water she bathes her whole body. That is the steam pot.

Every day for seven days the pot is made ready from late afternoon to sunset, and she sits over it for an hour. She is glad when it is over, because she knows that she will soon be reduced. When the pot treatment is finished, they make ready for the reduction, saying to the doctor, "She is your patient; tell your other patients that we are going to hold a dance." The husband goes to the shop to buy the spirit clothes, red cloth, black calico, and white muslin. Trousers are made of the white and the red, and a hut is built either in the town or outside.[5] It is called a *kilinge.*

At sunset the woman is taken to the kilinge, and there a platter is made ready. In it are placed bananas, sugar, cane, raw eggs, bread, and all sorts of good food. At the time of evening prayer the possessed person has her face painted with black, white, and red spots, and then they start the sound to entice the spirit up to her head. They dance and sing the song of enticement:

I pray thee, O Lord,
Thou, O Lord,
Undo my fetters,
Thou, O Lord.

The people respond, singing for something like an hour. As the spirit rises, it shakes all her limbs. Then the doctor interrogates, that is, talks with the spirit; but what he says no one knows but the doctor and his patient.[6] The doctor orders the drum to be beaten hard, and the spirit rises to dance. The initiates dance, and the sound of the drum carries them away. Some of them fall down in the kilinge, and when they reach home they are themselves in need of reduction.

Whosoever takes part in such proceedings has to obey certain rules whether he is a doctor or not. A doctor or a person of importance in the town who comes to watch the dance should be given cooked rice in a cup to pour out in the kilinge as a sign of respectful greeting to the doctor. He takes off his cap and is given a stool to sit on.

This dance goes on day and night for seven days. If the spirit is a good dancer, it is given presents by the people; but these presents belong not to it but to the doctor, the drummers, and the piper, for everyone who attends to watch the dance brings some money. This is not compulsory but voluntary. Every time the drum is beaten, the spirit dances and the people put money on its head.

The sixth day is the day for the spirit to be named. This is the day of revelation on which it is disclosed whether it is or is not a spirit. It gives a demonic name that no one knows, and when it does so all are much pleased.[7]

The seventh day is the day of release. A goat is slaughtered on the shore, and all the spirits come together to drink the goat's blood. If anyone does not drink the blood, he is not possessed. When they see the others drinking the blood, the spirits rise into the heads of those into whose heads they have not yet risen. After drinking the blood, the spirit is carried home cured.[8]

Swahili women and some men believe in the spirits and that if a person is possessed it must be reduced. If a woman is sick, she says to her husband, "Have me reduced." If he does not, there is endless trouble in the house, and she gets thinner and thinner. Men do their own reduction when they are possessed. Others say it is nonsense.

I once had an illness of the back and limbs, and a doctor was called in to treat me. He brought me Dungumaro steam for seven days.[9] Then he said to my parents, "Mtoro has the Dungumaro; do not let him eat mutton or anything fried with onions." My parents believed him. One day he said, "He is all right now; but let us reduce him so that the spirit lets him rest." My parents agreed, but when my teacher heard that I was to be reduced, he forbade me, saying, "Are you not ashamed to dance in the yard in the sight of everybody?" I was ashamed, and I told my parents that I would not be reduced. My mother was much frightened by my refusal, and when the doctor heard it, he said that I must not eat mutton and that if I did so I should die.

One day my teacher was asked to a party and I with him. The Arab host had killed a sheep, and my teacher said to me, "This is mutton; are you going to eat it?" I said I did not know, and he said, "Put your trust in God; there is no spirit; it is nonsense." I ate the mutton, and when I went home I told my mother that I had done so. She was horrified and said, "Why did you do that? Do you not value your life?" I waited for five or six days and had no pain from head to foot, and now here I am in Berlin.

Of Spirit Dances

THE KINYAMKERA SPIRIT

There are many different sorts of spirit; but the first and most important of all is Kinyamkera, originally a pagan spirit.[1] They believe that it lives on the tops of hills. When a person goes there he falls ill in his head or eyes or belly. If other treatment fails, he is treated for Kinyamkera, that is, with Kinyamkera vapors. These are made of dry leaves. Each spirit has its own vapor, but all are made of leaves, which are heated on a potsherd to fumigate the patient, the vapor penetrating the patient's limbs. This is the fumigation, and if he or she recovers it is clear that he or she was affected by a Kinyamkera spirit.

When the person is well, the husband says to the doctor, "Hold your patient by the ear and keep up her strength, and next year we will hold the reduction." The doctor speaks with the spirit and asks it for respite for a year.[2]

The reduction of Kinyamkera: When the doctor is ready for the reduction, he calls his female initiates and drummers—"On such a day I am holding a reduction, bring your drums."[3]

The initiates are women who have been possessed; but they have been treated, and the spirit has risen into their heads. When they went to the kilinge and the drums were beaten, the spirit rose into their heads. Or if she is at home and wants her spirit to come, she fumigates herself, and it rises into her head. If it has anything to say, the spirit speaks, and the people present hear. When the spirit leaves her, the people say, "Your spirit came today, and this is what it said," because she herself does not know.

The man buys the necessaries for Kinyamkera—bananas, cane, and eggs. At night the woman is taken into the country, where the drummers are ready. The dogori drums for Kinyamkera are seven: three *kirungura* placed together and played by one person with thin sticks. The fourth is a big dogori, the fifth a metal tray, and the sixth and seventh are chapuo. A chapuo is a double-ended drum.[4] When the drummers are ready, the possessed person first has her head shaved, then her face is daubed with red ocher, white gypsum, and soot in spots all over.

At these dances a log is set on fire and kept burning day and night. It is there by day also because its heat dries taut the drums. Every hour, a single rhythm is given, and the drums are heated because they have grown slack. The drummers bring them to the fire and tighten them up. Then when they are beaten they can be heard a long way off.

The sick person dances with the others for the appointed period, whether three or seven days, and the doctor sings:

You, my girl,
We will beat the tattoo for it.

They respond, and every hour the rhythm is changed and there is a different song such as:

Kinyamhunga,
None like you,
Kinyamhunga.[5]

When the dogori drumming is finished and the time has

come to break off, they make seven loaves of sorghum and six of ash with bits of cane and egg and chicks and roast sorghum. The patient puts on her head an empty flat basket and runs to her release under a baobab tree. The others, the doctor and the rest, follow her, carrying the things. When she reaches the tree, she falls down screaming. The doctor takes his patient by the chest and sings the song of release—"Come forth, Sengwa."

The people respond:

Come forth, Sengwa, O come forth, O come forth, O.

The patient screams loudly as the spirit is about to come forth, and when the release is complete, the chicken is killed, and the little loaves of sorghum and ash are placed at a fork in the road. A little roast sorghum is scattered at the fork with the words "This is your food, Kinyamkera." Then they take the sick person home, and in the morning they wash her face and limbs. The doctor is given a fee of a dollar to a dollar and a half. The drummers have a dollar between them.

NOTES TO APPENDIX II

Of Dances for Enjoyment

1. *Jumbe* may be translated "chief" and *ujumbe* "chieftaincy." In the Bagamoyo context it signified a member of one of the old "royal" families who partook of certain corporate sacral functions going back to ancient times and also exercised some political power. The title has to be distinguished from *mwinyi,* which often signifies "possessor" or "master" (as a title) or is perhaps the remnant of an older form of government. In German East Africa the term *jumbe* came to include such posts as *mwangi, mtemi, mwami,* and *mkulungwa.*

2. Something may be discerned in this ngoma kuu (great dance) of the elements of Bagamoyo society. A slave may not dance, though a woman slave attendant may circle with a chief. If a slave plays, he does so with bare head and feet. The freemen (the proud *waungwana)* are prominent, the shaha and waziri who have inherited or attained special status have their place, then come the jumbes.

3. This dance appears to have been danced by factions who sang antiphonally, litanywise (in this case the Mtondoo people and the Sitirihali folk). They seem to have consisted of two general lines or shallow crescents of people facing one another, each line dancing back and forth or sending out "champions" who confronted the other side. Here we see how closely some dances approximate ritual battles.

4. The *chapuo* is a double-ended drum; the *mrungura* is a long drum; the pipe is a like a reed flute; and the sound of the playing on a metal tray can be imagined, in that these days a *debe*, a five-gallon metal drum for carrying gasoline, with some stones in it, can be shaken in time with the music.

5. "Unyanyembe"—the country of the Wanyamwezi, capital Tabora (Kaze) or Urambo, at the junction of the routes to Lake Victoria and Lake Tanganyika. Swahili traders reached it fairly early in their travels

and used it as a base for their expeditions into the Congo and Buganda.

6. We see here stated on an elemental level the basic human need for factionalism and competition, a need that has generated such diverse events as the rivalry between "houses" artificially set up by the masters in Arnold's English public-school system, the family plague that beset the late medieval Italian cities so starkly portrayed in *Romeo and Juliet,* and the civil war that destroyed European hegemony in 1914–18. To sing, dance, and potlatch out hostility seem more enjoyable ways to ruin. Among the Enga of Highland New Guinea, for example, this type of quasi-warfare takes the form of the "pig exchange," though in some years actual warfare reemerges.

7. *Pishi* of rice—about four pints or six pounds.

8. Fungate—a part of the wedding celebrations, mentioned above. There is a hint here of a pre-Islamic seven-day week. Gongoni is a quarter of Bagamoyo.

9. *Kolekole* and *kowana*—fish, known for stupidity or other such qualities, used here as names for the opposite group.

10. "Like you"—this English translation is ambiguous; the meaning is closer to "similar to." This is apparently the song of a woman being divorced by her husband.

11. These are islands off the coast of East Africa.

12. In this dance the women of Swahili society appear in their appropriate functions and ranks—maiden, initiate, initiator-tutrix, and married woman. There are both African and Arab dances in which very old women played an essential role, but these are not mentioned here.

13. In this verse we may suppose a young woman begs her lover not to rush ahead to sexual intercourse, because all may be ruined by such haste.

14. "Learning" is *elimu*—Islamic higher studies beyond Qur'ān.

15. The kigori is the girl who has not yet been recognized as having had her first menstrual period. Once she is so recognized, she begins the education of initiation and becomes a mwari. A girl's first ovum may become fertilized if she is having regular sexual intercourse, but beyond this the song speaks of the feelings of any young woman, no matter the calendar age, who finds herself pregnant before she feels ready for children.

16. Velten takes this to be the lament of a man who has been committing adultery and hears from his wife that she has done the same. Innumerable folk songs from England and the United States contain this common theme of the (usually) woman's sorrow that her lover has coldly packed his bags.

17. Mkwaja is a place between Pangani and Sadan.

Of Spirits

1. The word translated "spirits" is *pepo. Spirits* is hardly a perfect term but is the best we have, for *compulsion-neurosis* or *hysteria* and the like are even worse. Attendance at seances and observation of the manifestations of such spirits lead one to think that they are things (denizens?) of the mind which are released or brought into being by certain factors; they are objective in a sense, controllable—or excitable—by people or factors outside one's own mind.

The extensive reading matter available on spirit possession and its dances includes R. Skene, "Arab and Swahili Dances and Ceremonies," *Journal of the Royal Anthropological Institute* 47 (1917): 413-434; H. Koritschoner, "Ngoma ya Shaitani, an East African Native Treatment for Psychical Disorders," *Journal of the Royal Anthropological Institute* 66 (1936): 209-219. John Beattie and John Middleton's *Spirit Mediumship and Society in Africa* (London, 1969) may be supplemented by reference to I. I. Zaretsky and C. Shambaugh, *Spirit Possession and Mediumship in Africa and Afro-America: An*

Annotated Bibliography (London, n.d.). Farouk Tharia Topan's distinguished 1971 London thesis, "Oral Literature in a Ritual Setting: The Role of Spirit Songs in a Spirit-Mediumship Cult," is a full-scale exegesis of the rites using the Victor Turner paradigms.

2. "Hold polytheistic beliefs in male and female spirits"—the Swahili is *wameshiriki pepo.* The awesome and dreadful root *sh-r-k* is used, which indicates the ultimate sin, in Muslim eyes, of associating a person or thing with God. Mtoro clearly indicates his views here, and at the end he reiterates that he personally considers the pepo business poppycock.

3. "A spirit in need of reduction"—Swahili *kupunga pepo.* It would be easy for us to make the translation of this chapter more immediately intelligible but much less accurate by varying the English translations of these two words according to the context, for they have no real equivalent in European languages. They should be treated as technical terms, however, and always translated by the same words, even when this leads to somewhat strained English.

Those who believe in pepo clearly envisage them as in some sense sentient beings with whom it is possible to converse, but no distinction can be drawn between them and diseases or the cause of diseases, nor can distinction be drawn between the pepo and the patient. Therefore, any pepo may, like a fever, move from the limbs to the head, and it is usually wrong to describe a pepo as "entering" a person or being "driven out." When Mtoro speaks of putting money on the head of the pepo, we are tempted to translate this as on the head of the patient; but to do so obscures the fact that the pepo and the patient are one. At the end the pepo has not been "driven out": the pepo goes home in good health; but the person is different. He or she is now *mteja,* which has been translated "initiate." The pepo has *not* been removed. Regarding the verb *kupunga,* to translate it as "exorcise" seems quite incorrect, because it can be used equally of the pepo and the patient; but it is not easy to find a single English word to fit all contexts. The word "reduce" has been used: it may be understood simultaneously in its normal and its medical sense, and it is applicable to a pepo considered as a spirit, a disease, or a condition, as well as to the sufferer. The patient is reduced, not to his or her original condition, which can never be restored, but to a satisfactory condition in which he or she can resume everyday life (as mteja). (It is to be noted that Mtoro usually, but not invariably, makes the tacit assumption that the patient is a woman.)

The remark that pepo come where there is trouble between husband and wife is significant. The cult is a means by which the underdog or person who feels slighted can get redress; we may compare similar cults among the Hausa, the *zar* cult in Ethiopia, and some aspects of the *jok* cult in Acholi. There may be some connection between the appearance of such cults and the recent lessening in women's fullness of life—for instance, in places where a more strict legalistic interpretation of Islam has overtaken an African traditional system, or in the United States, where American women were "fluffed" after being removed from the jobs they held during World War II.

4. The raising of the pepo to the head, to which there are frequent references, has to be understood in a double sense. Insofar as the pepo has a local habitation, it means that the pepo is located in the head. Insofar as the pepo is incorporeal, it means that the symptoms rise to the head.

5. The word "patient" in this paragraph is a translation of *mteja,* which could well be translated "initiate." The color symbolism of white, red, and black, the painting, the change of clothes are all indicative of initiation. In the next paragraph we may note how closely the pepo and the patient are identified, for it is literally the pepo's face that is painted.

6. The word translated "patient" here is *mwele,* one normally used of a sick person. The next word translated "doctor" is *fundi,* which indicates an expert, a craftsman. This may be a master of ceremonies, not the officiating mganga. The conversation is reminiscent of the rigmarole one has to go through to talk down a drug "high" or try to understand someone whose brain has been addled by LSD.

7. It is impressive how objectively Mtoro has described the pepo cult.

Only in such phrases as "gives a demonic name" *(jina la kijini)* does he reveal his own deeply Islamized thinking. (At the end, however, he feels free to state his own opinion: for him it is balderdash.)

8. The drinking of blood is as repellent to a Swahili Muslim as it is to a Jew. In a cult like this, the very doing of something totally obnoxious is part of the remaking, the new birth, of the person concerned.

9. *Dungumaro*—this pepo is described in *Customs of the Swahili People*, p. 105 (V 155).

Of Spirit Dances

1. "Kinyamkera," or sometimes *Chamkera,* is more commonly used of the "dust devil." The verb *-kera* means to annoy, and it is considered quite a minor devil. The dust devil is thought to be a little devil that picks up scraps of sweet things. For that reason children are not allowed to eat such things while standing up.

"A pagan spirit," *kishenzi*—pagan almost in the original derogatory sense of "rustic." The differentiation of spirits is reminiscent of I Corinthians and Acts. Some German Christians said of their behavior with regard to the Nazi phenomenon, "We did not discern the spirits."

2. The top of the ear is taken between finger and thumb, and the spirit *in the head* is addressed. After the fumigation and the identification of the pepo, there is a pause while resources are collected to make the reduction possible.

3. "female initiates"—*wateja wake wanawake. Mteja* as noted above is sometimes to be translated "patient," but the scene is one of initiation and here "initiate" is better. The song "You, my girl" uses the word *mwari,* which is employed of "maiden" initiates in puberty ceremonies.

4. The dogori is a Zaramo drum.

5. These songs, like many throughout the book, are under Zaramo

influence, as Velten's notes indicate. "Kinyamhunga" is the Zaramo by-form of the name of this pepo. ("Sengwa," below, is another by-form.) The implication is that it is this pepo and none other that has come upon the person.

BIBLIOGRAPHY

Ross E. Dunn, with the assistance of Darren Bardell, Jennifer Honigman, and Laura Ryan, has updated the bibliography to include a comprehensive listing of works on Ibn Battuta's life, career, and book of travels.

Abdur Rahim. "Six Hundred Years After—in the Footsteps of Ibn Battuta in Andalusia." *Peshawar University Review* 51 (1973): 1-21.

Abercrombie, Thomas J. "Ibn Battuta: Prince of Travelers." Photographs by James L. Stanfield. *National Geographic* 180 (Dec. 1991): 3-49.

Ajayi, J. F. A., and Michael Crowther. *The History of West Africa,* vol. 1. New York, 1971.

Allouche, Adel. "A Study of Ibn Battutah's Account of his 726/1326 Journey through Syria and Arabia." *Journal of Semitic Studies* 35 (1990): 283-99.

Arno, Joan, and Grady, Helen. "Ibn Battuta: A View of the Fourteenth-Century World, A Unit of Study for Grades 7-10." Los Angeles: National Center for History in the Schools, UCLA, 1998.

Asad, M. N. M. Kamil. "Ibn Battutah's Account of Malabar and Saylan (Sri Lanka)." *Journal of the Pakistan Historical Society* 42 (1994): 329-39.

Barth, H. *Travels and Discoveries in North and Central Africa.* New York, 1857. Reprint, London, 1965.

Beckingham, Charles F. "From Tangier to China—14th Century." *Hemisphere: An Asian-Australian Magazine,* 8 August 1978, 26-31.

_____. "Ibn Battuta in Sind." In *Sind Through the Centuries: Proceedings of an International Seminar, Karachi, 1975.* Edited by Hamida Khuhro. Karachi, 1981, 139-42.

_____. "In Search of Ibn Battuta." *Asian Affairs* 8 (1977): 263-77.

_____. "The Rihla: Fact or Fiction?" In I. R. Netton, ed. *Golden Roads: Migration, Pilgrimage and Travel in Mediaeval and Modern Islam.* Richmond, England, 1993, pp. 86-94.

Benjamin of Tudela. *The Itinerary.* Trans. and ed. by Marcus Nathan Adler. London, 1907. Reprint, New York, 1964.

Bhatnagar, R. "Madhyadesh in the Rehla of Ibn Battuta." *Saugar University Journal* 4 (1955-56): 97-109.

Bovill, Edward William. *The Golden Trade of the Moors: West African Kingdoms in the Fourteenth Century.* Oxford, 1958. Reprint ed., Princeton, 1995.

Bousquet, G. H. "Ibn Battuta et les Institutions Musulmanes." *Studia Islamica* 24 (1966): 81-106.

Bro, Thyge C. *Ibn Battuta: En arabisk rejsende fra det 14. århundrede.* Oslo, 2001. In Danish.

Brockelmann, Carl. *Geschichte der Arabischen Literatur, 2 den Supplementbaenden.* 2 vols. Leiden, 1943-49.

Bullis, Douglas. "The Longest Hajj: The Journeys of Ibn Battuta." *Saudi Aramco World* 51 (July/August 2000): 2-39.

Carim, Faud. *Marco Polo ve Ibn Battuta.* Istanbul, 1966.

Chelhod, Joseph. "Ibn Battuta, Ethnologue." *Revue de l'Occident Musulman et de la Méditerranée* 25 (1978): 5-24.

Chittick, H. Neville. *Kilwa: An Islamic Trading City on the East African Coast.* 2 vols. Nairobi, 1974.

_____. "Ibn Battuta and East Africa." *Journal de la Société des Africanistes* 38 (1968): 239-41.

Conermann, S. *Die Beschriebung Indiens in der "Rihla" des Ibn Battuta: Aspekte einer Herrschaftssoziologischen Einordnung des Delhi-Sultanates unter Muhammad Ibn Tugluq.* Berlin: Schwarz, 1993.

Cooley, W. D. *The Negrolands of the Arabs.* 1841. Reprint ed., London, 1966.

Cuoq, J. M. *Recueil des Sources Arabes Concernant l'Afrique Occidentale du VIIIe au XVIe Siècle.* Paris, 1975.

Dalziel, J. M. *The Useful Plants of West Tropical Africa.* London, 1937.

Defrémery, C., and B. R. Sanguinetti, eds. *Voyages d'Ibn Batoutah.* 3d ed. 4 vols. Paris, 1893-95.

Dulaurier, Edouard. "Description de l'Archipel d'Asie, par Ibn Bathoutha." *Journal Asiatique,* 4th ser., 9 (1874): 93-134, 218-59.

Dunn, Ross E. *The Adventures of Ibn Battuta, A Muslim Traveler of the 14th Century.* Rev. ed. Berkeley: University of California Press, 2004.

_____. "Migrations of Literate Muslims in the Middle Periods: The Case of Ibn Battuta." In I. M. Netton, ed., *Golden Roads: Migration, Pilgrimage and Travel in Mediaeval and Modern Islam.* London: Curzon Press, 1993.

_____. "Ibn Battuta and the Islamic World System." In *Ibn Battuta: Actes du Colloque International.* Tangier: L'École Supérieure Roi Fahd de Traduction, 1996, 41-48.

Eickelman, Dale F., and James Piscatori. *Muslim Travelers: Pilgrimage, Migration and the Religious Imagination.* Los Angeles, 1990.

Elad, Amikam. "The Description of the Travels of Ibn Battuta in Palestine: Is It Original?" *Journal of the Royal Asiatic Society* 2 (1987): 256-72.

El Moudden, Abderrahmane. "The Ambivalence of Rihla: Community Integration and Self-Definition in Moroccan Travel Accounts, 1300-1800." In Dale F. Eickelman and James Piscatori, eds., *Muslim Travelers: Pilgrimage, Migration, and the Religious Imagination.* Berkeley, 1990, pp. 69-84.

Fanjul, Serafin. "Elementos Folkloricos en la Rihla de Ibn Battuta." *Revista del Instituto Egipico de Estudios Islamicos en Madrid* 21 (1981-82): 153-79.

Fanjul, Serafin, and Frederico Arbós, trans. and eds. *Ibn Battuta a Través del Islam.* Madrid, 1981.

Ferrand, Gabriel. *Relations de Voyages et Textes Géographiques Arabes, Persans, et Turks Relatif à l'Extrême-Orient du VIII au XVIII siecles.* 2 vols. Paris, 1913-14.

Filipowiak, M. "L'expédition Archéologique Polono-Guinéene à Niani en 1968." *Africana Bulletin* 11 (1969): 107-117.

Fisher, A. G. B., and H. J. Fisher. *Slavery and Muslim Society in Africa.* London, 1970.

Freeman-Grenville, G. S. P. "Ibn Battuta's Visit to East Africa, a Translation." *Uganda Journal* 19 (1955): 1-6.

_____. *The Medieval History of the Coast of Tanganyika.* London, 1962.

_____. *The East African Coast.* Oxford, 1962.

Gabrieli, Francesco, trans. and ed. *I Viaggi di Ibn Battuta.* Florence, 1961.

Gibb, H. A. R. *Selections from the Travels of Ibn Battuta in Asia and Africa, 1325–1354.* London, 1929.

_____. "Notes sur les Voyages d'Ibn Battuta en Asie Mineure et en Russie." *Études d'Orientalisme Dediées à la memoire de Lévi-Provençal.* 2 vols. Paris, 1962, 1: 125–33.

_____, ed. *The Travels of Ibn Battuta A.D. 1325–1354, Translated with Notes from the Arabic Text Edited by C. Defremery and B. R. Sanguinetti.* 5 vols. Vols. 1–3: Cambridge University Press for the Hakluyt Society, 1958, 1961, and 1971. Vol. 4: Translation completed with annotations by C.F. Beckingham. London: Hakluyt Society, 1994. Vol. 5: Index, A. D. H. Bivar, compiler. Aldershot, England: Ashgate Publishing, 2001.

_____, trans. and ed. *Ibn Battuta: Travels in Asia and Africa.* 1929. Reprint ed., London, 1983.

_____, ed. *Islams Vandringsman: Ibn Battuta "Araboarldens Marco Polo" 1325–1354.* Stockholm, 1989.

Gies, Frances Carney. "To Travel the Earth." *Aramco World Magazine,* Jan.–Feb. 1978, 18–27.

Haig, M. R. "Ibnu Batuta in Sindh." *Journal of the Royal Asiatic Society 19* (1887): 393–412.

Hasan, Mehdi. "The *Rihla* of Ibn Battuta." *Proceedings of the Second Indian Historical Congress* (1938): 278–85.

Henke, K. "Ibn Batuta Berichtet über Chinesisches Papiergeld des 14 Jahrhunderts." *Hamburger Beitrage zur Numismatik* 36–38/1982–1984 (1993): 47–55.

Hinz, W. *Islamische Masse und Gewichte.* Leiden, 1955.

Hiskett, M. *The Development of Islam in West Africa.* London, 1982.

Horton, Mark, and John Middleton. *The Swahili: The Social Landscape of a Mercantile Society.* Oxford, 2000.

Hourani, C. F. *Arab Seafaring.* Princeton, 1951.

Hrbek, Ivan. "The Chronology of Ibn Battuta's Travels." *Archiv Orientální* 30 (1962): 409–86.

Hughes, T. P. *Dictionary of Islam.* London, 1885.

Hunwick, J. O. "The Term *Zanj* and its Derivatives in a West African

Chronicle." In D. Dalby, ed. *Language and History in Africa.* New York, 1970.

_____. "The Mid-Fourteenth Century Capital of Mali." *Journal of African History* 14 (1973): 195–208.

Husain, Agha Mahdi. "Ibn Battuta, His Life and Work." *Indo-Iranica* 7 (1954): 6–13.

_____. "Manuscripts of Ibn Battuta's *Rihla* in Paris." *Journal of the Asiatic Society of Bengal* 20 (1954): 49–53.

_____. "Ibn Battuta and his *Rihla* in New Light." *Sind University Research Journal* 7 (1967): 22–32.

_____. "Date and Précis of Ibn Battuta's Travels with Observations." *Sind University Research Journal* 8 (1968): 95–108.

_____. "Studies in the *Tuhfatunnazzar* of Ibn Battuta and Ibn Juzayy." *Journal of the Asiatic Society of Bangladesh* 23 (1978): 18–49.

_____, trans. and ed. *The Rehla of Ibn Battuta.* Baroda, India, 1976.

Ibn Battuta: Actes du Colloque International. Tangier: L'École Supérieure Roi Fahd de Traduction, 1996.

"Ibn Battuta: Muslim Scholar and Traveler." *Calliope* 9 (April 1999). Entire issue.

Ibn Battuta. *Rihla Ibn Batuta.* Pref. by al-Bustani. Beirut, 1964.

_____. *Ibn Batutah's Account of Bengal.* Trans. by Harinath De and ed. by P. N. Ghosh. Calcutta, 1978.

_____. *A Través del Islam.* Introduction, translation and notes by S. Fanjul and F. Arbos. Madrid, 1987.

Ibn Hajar al-Askalani. *Al-durar al-kamina.* 4 vols. Hyderabad, India, 1929–31.

Ibn Khaldun. *The Muqaddima.* Trans. and ed. by F. Rosenthal. 3 vols. 2nd ed. New York, 1967.

Ibn al-Mukhtar. *Ta'rikh al-Fattash.* Trans. and ed. by O. Houdas and M. Delafosse. Paris, 1913.

Istram, Tor. *The King of Ganda.* Stockholm, 1944.

Izzeddin, Mehmed. "Ibn Battouta et la Topographie Byzantine." *Actes du VI Congrés Internationale des Études Byzantines,* vol. 2. Paris, 1951.

Janicsek, Stephen. "Ibn Battuta's Journey to Bulghar: Is It a Fabrication?" *Journal of the Royal Asiatic Society* (October 1929): 791–800.

Janssens, Herman F. *Ibn Batoutah, le voyageur de l'Islam.* Brussels, 1948.
Johnson, Marion. "The Cowrie Currencies of West Africa." *Journal of African History* 11 (1970): 17–49, 331–53.
Khan, Abdul Majed. "The Historicity of Ibn Batuta Re. Sham-Suddin Firuz Shah, the So-Called Balbani King of Bengal." *Indian Historical Quarterly* 18 (1942): 65–70.
King, Noel. *There's Such Divinity Doth Hedge a King.* London, 1960.
_____. "Kingship as Communication and Accommodation." In F. F. Bruce, ed. *Promise and Fulfillment.* Edinburgh, 1964.
_____. *Religions of Africa.* New York, 1970.
_____. *Christian and Muslim in Africa.* New York, 1971.
_____. "Reading Between the Lines of Ibn Battuta for the History of Religion in Black Africa." *Milla wa-milla* 19 (1979): 26–33.
Lane, E. W. *An Account of the Manners and Customs of the Modern Egyptians.* 2 vols. London, 1836.
Law, R. C. C. *The Horse in West African History.* Oxford, 1980.
Lee, Samuel, trans. and ed. *The Travels of Ibn Batuta.* London, 1929.
Leo Africanus. *Description de l'Afrique.* 2 vols. Trans. by A. Epaulard, T. Monod, H. Lhote, and R. Mauny. Paris, 1956.
Leva, A. Enrico. "Ibn Batuta Nell' Africa Nera." *Africa* 16 (1961): 169–77.
Lévi-Procençal, E. "Le Voyage d'Ibn Battuta Dans le Royaume de Grenade (1350)." *Mélanges Offerts à William Marçais.* Paris, 1950: 205–24.
Levtzion, Nehemia. *Ancient Ghana and Mali.* London, 1973.
_____. "The Thirteenth and Fourteenth Century Kings of Mali." *Journal of African History* 4 (1961): 341–53.
_____ and J. F. P. Hopkins, trans. and ed. *Corpus of Early Arabic Sources for West African History.* New York, 1981. Reprint, Princeton, 2000.
Lhote, H. "Recherches sur Takedda, ville décrite part le voyageur arabe Ibn Battouta et située en Aïr." *Bulletin de l'IFAN* 34 (1972): 429–70.
Mackintosh-Smith, Tim. *Travels with a Tangerine: A Journey in the Footnotes of Ibn Battutah.* London, 2001.
Mackintosh-Smith, Tim, ed. *The Travels of Ibn Battutah.* London: Picador, 2002.

"Mansa Musa: King of Mali." *Calliope* 9 (Sept.-Oct. 1999). Entire issue.

Mapelli, López E. "Escolio Sobre la Málaga de Ibn Battuta (1350)." *Boletin de la Real Academia de Córdoba* 65/126 (1994): 221-29.

Markwart, J. "Ein Arabischer Bericht über die Arktischen (Uralischen) Lander aus dem 10 Jahrhundert." *Ungaarische Jahrbucher* 4 (1924): 261-334.

Mattock, J. N. "Ibn Battuta's Use of Ibn Jubayr's *Rihla*. In R. Peters, ed. *Proceedings of the Ninth Congress of the Union Européene des Arabisants et Islamisants.* Leiden, 1981: 209-18.

_____. "The Travel Writings of Ibn Jubair and Ibn Batuta." *Glasgow Oriental Society Transactions* 21 (1965-66): 35-46.

Mauny, Raymond. *Tableau Géographique de l'Ouest Africain au Moyen Age.* Amsterdam, 1967.

Mauny, R., V. Monteil, A. Djenidi, S. Robert, and J. Devisse. *Extraits Tirés des Voyages d'Ibn Battuta.* Dakar, 1966.

Mazrui, Alamin M., and Ibrahim Noor Shariff. *The Swahili: Idiom and Identity of an African People.* Trenton, N.J., 1994.

Meillassoux, Claude. "L'Itineraire d'Ibn Battuta entre Walata et Malli." *Journal of African History* 13 (1972): 389-95.

Middleton, John. *African Merchants of the Indian Ocean: Swahili of the East African Coast.* Long Grove, Ill., 2004.

Miquel, André. "Ibn Battuta, Trente Années de Voyages de Pekin au Niger." *Les Africains* 1 (1977): 117-40.

_____. "L'Islam d'Ibn Battuta." *Bulletin d'Études Orientales* 30 (1978): 75-83.

Mirza, M. Wahid. "Khusrau and Ibn Battuta, a Comparative Study." In *Professor Muhammad Shafi' Presentation Volume.* Lahore, 1955: 171-80.

Mollat, Michel. "Ibn Batoutah et la Mer." *Travaux et Jours* 18 (1966): 53-70.

Moraes, G. M. "Haryab of Ibn Batuta." *Journal of the Bombay Branch of the Royal Asiatic Society* 15 (1938): 37-49.

Morris, J. "Ibn Batuta: The Travels and the Man." *Ur* (1980): 23-27.

Monrat, M. "Notice sur l'Emplacement de l'Ancienne Capitale du Mali." *Notes Africaines* 79: 90-93.

Monteil, C. *Les Empires du Mali.* Paris, 1939. Reprint ed., 1968.

Monteil, Vincent. "Introduction aux Voyages d'Ibn Battuta (1325-53)." *Bulletin de l'IFAN* 30, series B, no. 2 (1968): 444-62.

Murdock, A. P. *Africa, Its People and Their Cultural History.* New York, 1959.

N'Diaye, Aissatou. "Sur la Transcription des Vocables Africains par Ibn Baththutah." *Notes Africaines* 38 (1948): 26-27.

Netton, Ian Richard. "Myth, Miracle and Magic in the *Rihla* of Ibn Battuta." *Journal of Semitic Studies* 29 (1984): 131-40.

_____. "Arabia and the Pilgrim Paradigm of Ibn Battuta: A Braudelian Approach." *Arabia and the Gulf: From Traditional Society to Modern State. Essays in Honour of M. A. Shaban's 60th birthday (16th November, 1986).* Ed. by I. R. Netton. London, 1986.

_____. "Tourist *Adab* and Cairene Architecture: The Medieval Paradigm of Ibn Jubayr and Ibn Battutah." *Literary Heritage of Classical Islam: Arabic and Islamic Studies in Honor of James A. Bellamy.* Ed. by Mustansir Mir in Collaboration with J. E. Fossum. Princeton, 1993.

_____, ed. *Golden Roads: Migration, Pilgrimage and Travel in Mediaeval and Modern Islam.* Richmond, England, 1993.

Niane, D.T. *Recherches sur l'Empire du Mali au Moyen Age.* Conakry, 1962.

_____. *Sundiata, an Epic of Old Mali.* Trans. by C. D. Pickett. London, 1965.

_____. "Le Probleme de Soundiata." *Notes Africaines* 88: 123-27.

Norris, H.T. "Ibn Battutah's Andalusian Journey." *Geographical Journal* 125 (1959): 185-96.

_____. "Ibn Battuta's Journey in the North-Eastern Balkans." *Journal of Islamic Studies* 5 (1994): 209-20.

Nurse, Derek, and Thomas Spear. *The Swahili: Reconstructing the History and Language of an African Society, 800-1500.* Philadelphia, 1984.

Papin, Y. D. "Ibn Battuta: Le Plus Grand Voyageur Médiéval." *Archeologia* 165 (1982): 81-85.

Park, Mungo. *Travels in the Interior Districts of Africa.* London, 1815.

Polo, Marco. *The Travels of Marco Polo.* Trans. by Ronald Latham. Baltimore, 1958.

Pouwells, Randall. *Horn and Crescent: Cultural Change and Traditional Islam on the East African Coast, 800–1900.* Cambridge, 1987.

Rashid, Abdur. "India and Pakistan in the Fourteenth Century as Described by Arab Travelers." In *Congresso internacional de Historia Dos Descobrimentos.* Lisbon, 1961.

Rawlinson, H. G. "The Traveller of Islam." *Islamic Culture* 5 (1931): 29–37.

Robert, D. S., and J. Devisse. *Tegdaoust I, Recherches sur Aoudaghost.* Paris, 1970.

Quiros Rodriquez, C. "B. Batuta: un Viajero Tangerino sel Siglo XIV." *Archivos del Instituto de Estudios Africanos* 6 (1952): 11–27.

Al-Sadi. *Ta'rikh al-Fattash.* Trans. by O. Houdas. Paris, 1911.

Saletore, R. N. "Haryab of Ibn Battuta and Harihara Nrpala." *Quarterly Journal of the Mythic Society* 31 (1940–41): 384–406.

Schacht, J. *Introduction to Islamic Law.* Oxford, 1964.

Seco de Lucena, Luis. "De Toponimia Granadina: Sobre el Vije de Ibn Battuta al Reino de Granada." *Al-Andalus* 16 (1951): 49–85.

Shelton, A. S. "The Problem of *griot* Interpretation." *Présence Africaine* 116 (1968): 145–52.

de Slane, M. G. "Traduction des Passages Relatifs au Soudan." *Journal Asiatique* 5 (March 1843): 181–246.

Sobret, J. "Les Frontières chez Ibn Battuta." In *Actes du 8ème Congrés de l'Union Européenne des Arabisants et Islamisants.* Aix-en-Provence, 1978, 305–308.

Stewig, R. "Versuch Einer Auswertung der Reisebeschreibung von Ibn Battuta (Nach der Englischen Ubersetzung von H. A. R. Gibb) zur Bedeutungs-Differenzierung Westanatolischer Siedlungen." *Der Islam* 47 (1971): 43–58.

Trimingham, Spencer J. *Islam in the Sudan.* Oxford, 1949.

_____. *Islam in West Africa.* Oxford, 1959.

_____. *A History of Islam in West Africa.* Oxford, 1962.

Von Mzik, Hans, trans. and ed. *Die Reise des Arabers Ibn Batuta durch Indien und China.* Hamburg, 1911.

Charles-Dominique, P., trans. and ed. *Voyageurs Arabes.* Paris, 1985.

Yamamoto, T. "On Tawalisi as Described by Ibn Battuta." *Memoirs of*

the Research Department of the Toyo Bunko 8 (1936): 93–133.
Yule, Henry. *Cathay and the Way Thither.* 4 vols. London, 1913–16.
Yule, Henry, and A. C. Burnell. *Hobson-Jobson.* 1886. Reprint ed., London, 1970.
Zemp, H. "La Légende des *Griots* Malinkes." *Cahiers d'Éudes Africaines* 7: 611–42.

INDEX TO THE TRANSLATION

9 781558 763364